Ethnic and Intercommunity Conflict Series

General Editors: **Seamus Dunn**, Professor of Conflict Studies and Director, Centre for the Study of Conflict, and **Valerie Morgan**, Professor of History and Research Associate, Centre for the Study of Conflict, University of Ulster, Northern Ireland

With the end of the Cold War, the hitherto concealed existence of a great many other conflicts, relatively small in scale, long-lived, ethnic in character and intra- rather than inter-state has been revealed. The dramatic changes in the distribution of world power, along with the removal of some previously resolute forms of centralised restraint, have resulted in the re-emergence of older, historical ethnic quarrels, many of which either became violent and warlike or teetered, and continue to teeter, on the brink of violence. For these reasons, ethnic conflicts and consequent violence are likely to have the greatest impact on world affairs during the next period of history.

This new series examines a range of issues related to ethnic and intercommunity conflict. Each book concentrates on a well-defined aspect of ethnic and intercommunity conflict and approaches it from a comparative and international standpoint.

Rather than focus on the macrolevel, that is on the grand and substantive matters of states and empires, this series argues that the fundamental causes of ethnic conflict are often to be found in the hidden roots and tangled social infrastructures of the opposing separated groups. It is through the understanding of these foundations and the working out of their implications for policy and practical activity that may lead to ameliorative processes and the construction of transforming social mechanisms and programmes calculated to produce longterm peace.

Titles include:

Stacey Burlet
CHALLENGING ETHNIC CONFLICT

Ed Cairns and Mícheál Roe (*editors*)
THE ROLE OF MEMORY IN ETHNIC CONFLICT

T.G. Fraser
THE IRISH PARADING TRADITION

Tony Gallagher
EDUCATION IN DIVIDED SOCIETIES

Colin Knox and Padraic Quirk
PEACE BUILDING IN NORTHERN IRELAND, ISRAEL AND SOUTH AFRICA

Colin Knox and Rachel Monaghan
INFORMAL JUSTICE IN DIVIDED SOCIETIES
Northern Ireland and South Africa

Brendan Murtagh
THE POLITICS OF TERRITORY

Marc H. Ross
THEORY AND PRACTICE IN ETHNIC CONFLICT MANAGEMENT

Education in Divided Societies

Tony Gallagher
Professor of Education
Queen's University Belfast

palgrave
macmillan

First published 2004 by
PALGRAVE MACMILLAN
Houndmills, Basingstoke, Hampshire RG21 6XS and
175 Fifth Avenue, New York, N. Y. 10010
Companies and representatives throughout the world

PALGRAVE MACMILLAN is the global academic imprint of the Palgrave Macmillan division of St. Martin's Press, LLC and of Palgrave Macmillan Ltd. Macmillan® is a registered trademark in the United States, United Kingdom and other countries. Palgrave is a registered trademark in the European Union and other countries.

ISBN 0–333–67708–0

This book is printed on paper suitable for recycling and made from fully managed and sustained forest sources.

A catalogue record for this book is available from the British Library.

Library of Congress Cataloging-in-Publication Data
Gallagher, Tony.
    Education in divided societies / Tony Gallagher.
        p. cm. – (Ethnic and intercommunity conflict series)
    Includes bibliographical references and index.
    ISBN 0–333–67708–0
        1. Minorities–Education–Cross-cultural studies. 2. Multicultural education–Cross-cultural studies. 3. Ethnicity–Cross-cultural studies.
I. Title. II. Ethnic and intercommunity conflict series (Palgrave Macmillan (Firm))

LC3715.G35 2005
371.829–dc22   2004050895

10   9   8   7   6   5   4   3   2   1
13   12   11   10   09   08   07   06   05   04

Printed and bound in Great Britain by
Antony Rowe Ltd, Chippenham and Eastbourne

Contents

Foreword and Acknowledgements

This book has been long in gestation and there have been many people along the way who have supported and inspired me in various ways. Perhaps the most important of these were Karen Trew, for her work on the psychology of conflict, Bob Cormack and Bob Osborne, for their work on equality, and John Darby and Seamus Dunn, for their work on conflict and conflict resolution. I owe a great debt to all of them. Needless to say, while they have inspired work which has contributed to this book, I am solely responsible for its contents.

This book is based on a search for a way in which education can make a positive and progressive contribution to societies that are undergoing ethnic conflict. To a large part the reason for thinking about this issue arises from my own experience of growing up in Northern Ireland during the most violent part of its history.

The book is really organised around four themes. The first concerns the nature of conflict between people and is examined in the first three chapters. The experience of the Holocaust is examined first as a reminder of the depths to which human depravity can sink, but it is a reminder also that this should not be seen simply as a reversion to some sort of barbarous primitivism. The Holocaust, in other words, is a consequence of modernity, not an abandonment of it. The next two chapters examine the social processes that have created ethnically plural societies and some strands of work with Social Psychology which have attempted to offer some framework of understanding for these phenomena.

The second theme, covering the next four chapters, begins our examination of the impact of different educational structures. Chapter 4 looks at the three most plural European states, all of which operate federalised political systems in which education decision-making is a largely decentralised activity. The next three chapters examine the experience of the United States and Great Britain, both of which have tried to operate a common school system in which education is used primarily to promote social integration.

The third theme, covering the next two chapters, examines two situations where education is divided. The first of these is provided by apartheid South Africa in which education played a key role in the maintenance of minority White rule. The second is provided by

Northern Ireland where parallel religious school systems operate for Protestants and Catholics.

In the final chapter we try to draw the various strands of experience examined in the book together to see what can be learned for future practice. The main arguments we conclude with are that, for good or ill, there is no educational structure that provides a guaranteed positive (or negative) outcome, but that what is needed is a process of dialogue to determine what is considered desirable as educational outcomes and a willingness to act towards those outcomes.

For me the example of Northern Ireland hangs over the discussion throughout this book. It is in Northern Ireland that I live and work and it is there I can best make a contribution to the development of an educational system.

This book is dedicated to Liam Canning, a young man, a friend, who died in Northern Ireland and of whom I think almost every day.

1
The Holocaust

The murder of the Jews

On January 27, 1945, Soviet troops pursuing the German army west-wards came upon a place that defied human imagination. The place was called Auschwitz. Since 1942 between one and two million people had been gassed and incinerated in the camp. Most of those who died were Jews and died because they were Jews. The Holocaust, or Shoah, stands as a horrible monument to inhumanity and the consequence of prejudice.

The Nazi Party had its origins in the confusion and instability fol-lowing the end of the First World War and based its support on the exploitation of popular opposition to the Versailles Peace Treaty. The Nazis were not the only political group that built a platform on mili-tant nationalism (Noakes and Pridham, 1983), nor was it the only group which advocated anti-Semitism (Hilberg, 1985; Litvinoff, 1989), but during the 1920s and early 1930s the Nazis consolidated opposi-tion to the Weimar Republic until they came to power in 1933. Once in power they used this position to purge political opponents (Noakes and Pridham, 1983: p. 136) with a determination and single-minded-ness that stood in stark contrast to the vacillation of their opponents. Traditional anti-Semitism cast the Jews as the 'killers of Christ' and left open the option of forced or voluntary conversion.

The form of anti-Semitism that developed in the nineteenth and early twentieth centuries built on these traditional religious founda-tions, but added Darwinian notions of the survival of the fittest, and Mendelian ideas on genetic transmission and heredity. One result was the popularisation of eugenics, the notion that states not only could, but should, manipulate the genetic endowment of their populations in order to encourage the reproduction of the 'fittest' and discourage the reproduction of the 'least fit'. Another result was the promulgation of a 'quasi-scientific' anti-Semitism which, being rooted in biological determinism, foreclosed the option of conversion as a solution to the 'Jewish problem' (Kohn, 1995). The brutal logic of biological determinism meant that expulsion or destruction were left as the only options for action.

The actions of the Nazis against Jews proceeded in stages. A series of laws were passed to dismiss Jews from civil service and later all public service occupations, while the Nuremburg Laws (1935) removed all citizenship rights from Jews (Arad et al., 1981). Mass action by Nazi party members included organised boycotts of Jewish businesses and attacks on Jewish property. Following the most systematic destruction of Jewish property on Kristellnacht (November, 1938) thousands of Jews were arrested and the community fined. Jews were encouraged to emigrate and special offices were established to enable these measures, initially in Austria after the Anchluss, and later in Germany as a whole. Throughout 1939 and 1940, after the invasion of Poland, it seemed that the expulsion of the Jews from territory under Nazi control through emigration remained the predominant and preferred strategy. However, in October 1941, an order was issued by Himmler, head of the SS and Chief of Security Police, banning all further emigration of Jews out of Nazi-controlled territory. By this time it seems clear that a decision had been taken to pursue a more brutal solution to the 'Jewish problem'.

The roots of this solution can be traced to an earlier programme directed against 'mental defectives' during which the Nazi state murdered almost 100,000 mentally ill patients in a euthanasia programme (Noakes and Pridham, 1986: pp. 997–1048). This programme operated between 1939 and 1945, and became increasingly formalised in the identification and processing of victims, leading to the search for more 'efficient' methods of killing. Although legal authorities became aware of the euthanasia programme because some of the patients were wards of court, few judges or public prosecutors protested. The Churches too were uncomfortably quiescent, anxious to avoid a confrontation with the state. It is noteworthy also that the Nazis tried to establish a favourable public climate for euthanasia, presumably preparing for a day when the programme could be legally and openly followed (Burleigh and Wippermann, 1991; Lifton, 1986).

After the seizure of Poland, in addition to the new territory, the Reich also acquired control over several million more Jews. Regulations meant that all Jews had to wear identifying armbands, register with the authorities and were banned from moving without authorisation. By 1941 almost all had been concentrated in one of seven main ghettos in a region in the south and west of the country known as the General Government. When the Soviet Union was invaded in June 1941, it was clear that a decision had been made to kill all the Jews in the territory. Four special action squads, or Einsatzgruppen, were established to follow the invasion. Their task was simply to round up Jews and any political officials they could find, and to shoot them. In the first sweep, up to December 1941, the Einsatzgruppen shot about 100,000 Jews a month, usually at mass graves on the outskirts of cities. Jewish communities bypassed by the Einsatzgruppen in the first wave of killings were concentrated in ghettos and these provided the victims for the second sweep that began in late 1941 and continued through the spring and summer of 1942 during which the ghettoes were systematically cleared. By the late summer of 1942 the task was almost complete. Raul Hilberg has estimated that the total number of Jews shot and killed during these operations came to a little over 1.3 million (Hilberg, 1985).

At some point in 1941, probably after the decision to kill Soviet Jews had been taken, a decision was taken to kill all the Jews of Europe as the 'final solution' to the 'Jewish problem', but the scale of this task required the construction of special 'factories of death', where modern industrial techniques were applied and the process for dealing with vast numbers of transferred people was bureaucratised (Hilberg, 1985). The Wansee Conference, which marked the final coordination of this murder-machine, identified the target as including not only Jews in the areas then under Nazi control, but also Jews in the rest of unoccupied Europe comprising a total of over ten million people (Arad et al., 1981: pp. 249–261; Noakes and Pridham, 1986: pp. 1125–1129).

Camps were established in Treblinka, Sobibor, Belzec and Chelmo with the sole purpose of killing everyone transported to them: in total as many as two million people may have entered these death camps, but as few as several hundred may have survived the war as witnesses. The more familiar camp established at Auschwitz contained a death facility, a concentration camp for political and other opponents of the regime and slave labour camps. In total, a million people or more were murdered in Auschwitz, but several tens of thousands survived as witnesses to the murders. In January 1945, the camp authorities attempted to destroy some of the camp facilities as Soviet troops approached and evacuated surviving prisoners by foot and train back towards the west, leaving behind several thousand who were believed to be close to death. Hundreds, if not thousands, died on the forced march westwards and many ended up in concentration and slave labour camps where they were discovered by horrified and disbelieving Allied troops (Abzug, 1985). The horror was sustained as, for many, liberation came too late and the ravages of disease and hunger continued to take their toll. Indeed in some cases the situation was even worse as Polish anti-Semitics murdered Jews who had escaped from camps in Poland after the war was over. It was hardly surprising, therefore, that many Jews who did survive decided to leave Europe for a new life in Israel, which was to declare independence in 1948.

Understanding the Holocaust?

Such is the unique character of the Holocaust that it almost defies explanation or understanding. In the immediate aftermath of the war, popular explanations were rooted either in the character of Germans, or German culture. This view seemed to underlie part of the prosecution case at the Nuremburg trials (Tusa and Tusa, 1983) and was given a popular basis by the journalist William Shirer (Shirer, 1959). Research by psychologists in the USA focused on the development of an anti-democratic personality type, the Authoritarian Personality, as the developmental cause of fascism (Adorno et al., 1950). Despite the weaknesses in these explanations based on individual psychology (see Billig, 1978), they continue to be drawn upon in what at times appear to be an overly eclectic manner (Staub, 1989). Rather than seeing the Holocaust as a regression to primitivism, other social scientists have argued that it should be seen as a consequence of modernity, rather than an aberration from modernity (Bauman, 1989). Thus, it is pointed out, mass murder on that scale was only possible if the process of death was mechanised, and that route was only available to a modern, twentieth-century, industrialised state.

Historians have their disputes over the Holocaust also. For some years there was a significant debate between 'intentionalists', who argued that the programme of mass murder had always been a core part of Nazi ideology, and the 'functionalists' who argued that the road to the Holocaust was much less even and comprised more the result of a myriad of bureaucratic responses to administrative problems rather than a long-term plan (for varying perspectives on this debate see, for example, Fleming, 1985; Mommsen, 1986; and Browning, 1992). Following this and as Marrus (1988) has pointed out, much less productively, was the Historians' debate in Germany. This was sparked by a claim that the Holocaust was a response to a real threat from the Soviet Union and was, in any case, no different from the mass killings of the 1930s purges under Stalin (see Weiss, 1988).

For the present we are content to focus on simpler issues. In the archives of Yad Vashem, the commemoration museum in Jerusalem, lies a photograph of two young Jewish boys. They stand in front of their German classmates, heads bowed, as their teacher tells the class of the perfidy of the Jews. The theme of his lesson is written on the blackboard. Within a decade, the two boys, or at least many like them, had been murdered and reduced to ashes by the logic of that same prejudice and discrimination. In total perhaps only several thousands of people were directly involved in the killing process, although hundreds of thousands were involved in the host of specific administrative tasks that enabled the transportation and murder of such large numbers of people. But for most non-Jewish people throughout Nazi-controlled Europe, their main experience was that Jews disappeared and few seemed to want to know what had happened to them. This is the conclusion arrived by William Sheridan Allen in his detailed examination of the experience of one German town during the Nazi period:

> By the time Hitler had determined to murder ... the Jews ... almost all of Nordheim's Jews had left the town for a bigger city and supposed anonymity. Nordheimers did not harass their Jewish neighbours, but they also did their best not to 'know' what their government was doing to the Jews. (Allen, 1989: pp. 290–291).

Ian Kershaw following his detailed examination of popular opinion in Bavaria put the same theme thus:

> Popular opinion, largely indifferent and infused with a latent anti-Jewish feeling further bolstered by propaganda, provided the climate within which spiralling Nazi aggression towards the Jews could take place unchallenged. But it did not provoke the radicalisation in the first place. The road to Auschwitz was built by hate, but paved by indifference. (Kershaw, 1984: p. 277).

It is this sense of indifference that should form the main theme or warning we take from the Holocaust. It involved one group of Europeans attempting to end the existence of another group of Europeans, with religion as the main marker of difference. It was possible both because those who wanted to impose death actively pursued their goal, and those who might ordinarily be expected to oppose such a measure, often did little or nothing. If the Holocaust could be explained in terms of a particular national group or cultural history then it would be easy to avoid in the future. If it is explained by indifference, or something akin to indifference, it could all too easily happen again.

The twentieth century was to be the bloodiest century in human history, with more people killed in wars than in all previous centuries combined. And towards the end of the century we were reminded again of the ease with which some people could find themselves pursuing the systematic slaughter of other people deemed to be different. The following account provides a more recent witness of a mass murder that held chilling echoes with the action of the Einsatzgruppen in the 1940s:

> In all, the squad dispatched fifteen to twenty busloads of men. Erdemovic estimated that some 1,200 men were killed in five and a half hours ... The terrified and horrified bus drivers were also made to kill at least one [victim], so that they would never be tempted to confess later. (Honig and Both, 1996: p. 64)

The events described here took place at a farm at the village of Pilica, which is near the town of Srebrenica. The mass killings were carried out on July 16, 1995, and involved one group of Europeans, Serbs, killing another group of Europeans, Bosnian Muslims, because of their religion. It would seem that we have yet to learn the lessons of history.

2
We Are All Ethnic Now

Introduction

The twentieth century has witnessed the end of empires and the rise of the nation-state, with new states emerging at the end of each of the First, Second and Cold Wars. The most spectacular growth occurred between 1945 and 1984 when the number of independent states rose from 72 to 168 (Kidron and Segal, 1984). The post-1945 expansion of states was linked to the decline of colonialism so that by 1984 there remained less than ten occupied or colonial territories across the globe. But despite the rise in the number of independent states, territorial boundaries have usually remained stable. Thus, between 1945 and 1984, the most significant territorial changes were the secession of East Pakistan to form Bangladesh, the forced partition of Cyprus, the reintegration of Vietnam, and Israeli occupation of the West Bank and Gaza Strip.

The end of the Cold War was marked by the continuation of these processes. The period immediately following the collapse of the communist states in Europe saw hitherto unimaginable change, with the unification of the two Germanys, the breakup of Czechoslovakia, the collapse of the USSR and the disintegration of Yugoslavia. Yet here too the international community has largely tried to deal with these changes within the context of existing territorial boundaries. This approach is motivated by a recognition of the difficulty of peacefully resolving territorial disputes, and a recognition of the mismatch between ethnicity and the existing states system in the world (Connor, 1972). This was the motivation behind the 1964 Cairo declaration of the Organisation of African Unity (OAU) Assembly of Heads of State and Government, which pledged states to respect borders on the achievement of national independence (Harding, 1993). Similar motives influenced a declaration by the Council for Security and Co-operation in Europe (CSCE) in 1991.

This contrasted with the Versailles settlement after the First World War when the winning powers deliberately tried to redraw the map of Europe to create ethnically more homogeneous states out of the ashes of the collapsed empires in Germany and Austro-Hungary. Prior to this, the received wisdom of state-craft in Europe favoured a balance-of-power approach in which a system of shifting alliances, or the occasional intervention by a balancing power, would ensure that no protagonist gained a predominant position. From this perspective a plethora of small states in Europe was undesirable as it would create a large number of weak states, many of which might be led by people who were ill-versed in diplomatic skills and increase the number of potential conflicts on the continent. But the thinking at Versailles was informed by a view of international diplomacy in which principal was to predominate over pragmatism. This approach was expressed most directly in President Wilson's Fourteen Points, but clearly influenced the thinking and approach of many of the officials involved in the negotiations, some of whom felt they were 'bent on doing great, permanent and noble things' (Nicholson, 1933). The rationale for this view was that the recognition of self-determination would create a continent of democratic states which would be 'naturally' peaceful, with little interest or motivation in conflict with their neighbours. Churchill (1929) argued that the idea had worked, largely because for the first time in European history the map conformed to the general wishes of the people. Writing at the other end of the century, however, Eric Hobsbawm (1994) adjudged Versailles as a failure as, not only had it failed to eliminate interstate conflict, but also it had failed to lay to rest the basis for interethnic conflict: 'The national conflicts tearing the continent apart in the 1990s were the old chickens of Versailles once again coming home to roost'. An adjunct deal tried to impose a similar punishment on the Ottoman Empire as the Treaty of Sèvres (1920) proposed the ceding of some Turkish territory to Greece, the demilitarisation and internationalisation of other parts of Turkey, the establishment of an independent Republic of Armenia and the creation of European mandates in parts of the Middle East. The Turkish nationalists under Kemal rejected the proposals and, after a short, but successful war against Greece, achieved major revisions in the Treaty of Lusannes (1923), but even this involved the forced transfer of over 1.3 million people.

The limited success of these post-Versailles territorial revisions, not least because of the fluidity of human settlement and the actual difficulty in creating ethnically homogeneous territory without significant, and usually enforced, population movements, at least partly explains the reluctance of the international community to countenance such 'solutions' in the later years of the twentieth century (Dunn and Fraser, 1996).

The twentieth century was also marked by attempts by the international community to establish a global basis for order, first through the League of Nations, later through the UN. This effort has had limited success. The League of Nations was established to promote collective security, provide a basis for arbitration in international disputes and sought to reduce armaments. Its failure to create a basis for these aims is best highlighted by the Second World War. But the ability of the UN to restrain conflict has been limited also. Between 1945 and 1988 there were 94 wars with estimated casualties of between 17–30 million, and, of these, 69 were general or regional civil wars. In the same period there were 208 successful coups or revolutions within states (Brogan, 1989) and in 1987 there remained some 80 border and territorial disputes between states (Day, 1987). The University of Uppsala has estimated that there were 82 armed conflicts in the world between 1989 and 1992, and 35 of these had casualties amounting to more than 1,000 deaths per year (Sollenberg and Wallensteen, 1995). In the latter years of the twentieth century the wars continued unabated. Increasingly, however, they were internal struggles rather than wars between states, the number of cases which involved external intervention was low, and the highest proportion of wars were found in Asia and, more particularly Africa (Seybolt, 2000; Sollenberg et al., 1999; Sollenberg and Wallensteen, 1998). This last aspect was attributed by Sollenberg and Wallenstein (1998) to the weakness of many African states and the fact that this became more evident after the end of the Cold War, something we consider further below.

There have always been sub-state groups using violence to achieve political, territorial or other ends, although most operated within state boundaries. In the latter half of the twentieth century some of these groups internationalised their campaigns to establish the era of international 'terrorism'. In 2002 the US State Department estimated that there had been an average of 350 acts of international terrorism per year throughout the 1990s, a fall from an average of 540 incidents per year in the 1980s, which was lower again than the peak period of recorded incidents in the early 1970s. Much of the attacks of interest to the State Department dealt with attacks on US citizens and, for a long period, the largest number, and hence most significant, were attacks in South America (see www.state.gov for general statistics and reports). However, the horrific attacks on the World Trade Center on September 11, 2001 changed the situation dramatically, with the US attempting to rally as many countries as possible behind an international campaign against international terrorism (http://www.state.gov/s/ct/rls/pgtrpt/2001/pdf/). Although most are at pains to argue that this new war of the twenty-first century is not between Christianity and Islam, there is undoubtedly a sense that these religious identities provide a significant element of the fault-lines for international conflict. It is as if the discourses on Christian/Islamic differences have replaced that provided for earlier generations by democracy/communism, in the twentieth century, and Catholicism/Protestantism, in the seventeenth century. That these identities are of any significance only serves again to reinforce the limitations of the modernist expectation invested in the nation-state.

These statistics of war and conflict highlight the rise of ethnicity, ironically at the end of the century that many believed marked the end of such particularistic identities and affiliations. Ethnicity, that is a sense of collective based on religion, language, culture or some other shared origin, was supposed to have been swept away by the tide of modernity. In this chapter we will examine just how mistaken this view proved to be and consider the resurgence of ethnicity not only as a practical reality, but also as a key concept in the attempt to understand the nature of social relationships. Our main interest lies in the period when ethnicity re-emerged as an issue of concern: in a relatively short period the literature in this area has burgeoned and there is no attempt made here to encompass it all.

The contemporary significance of ethnicity

Ethnicity has been demonstrating a new vitality at least since the 1970s. The collapse of the bipolar world was succeeded by an escalation of disputes between the successor countries of Yugoslavia and the USSR, while the re-emergence of ethnic tensions in Central and East Europe has highlighted the issue in other regions. The world witnessed upsurges of ethnic nationalism in South Asia and Southern Africa, of racial intolerance in some European countries and of religious fundamentalism in parts of the Middle East. Social and political conflicts in Latin America, notably in Nicaragua, Guatemala, Chile,

Peru and Colombia, deeply affected relationships between the indigenous peoples and the state (Rupesinghe and Tishkov, 1996).

The statistics highlight the growth of the phenomenon: thus, in the late 1970s, 18 states had significant internal linguistic conflicts and 19 had significant internal religious conflicts. In the mid-1980s, 76 states had active opposition groups organised around minority grievances, while a further 38 had evidence of minority grievances, but no organised opposition groups. In as many as 41 of these states, minority opposition groups used violent methods to press their claims (Kidron and Segal, 1984). The process continued in the 1990s and beyond: Darby (1997) estimated that in 1996 there were 74 active violent political conflicts, 19 of which had resulted in more than 1,000 deaths in that single year. The annual yearbooks of the Stockholm Peace Research Institute (SIPRI) suggested that, throughout the last decade of the twentieth century, there have been 56 active major armed conflicts in 44 different locations, all but three of which were intra-state conflicts (Sollenberg and Wallensteen, 2001). Of the 25 major armed conflicts in 2000, 12 had caused at least 1,000 battle-related deaths in that year, and most of these had an accumulated death total of over 30,000. At the century's end, the UN had 19 peacekeeping operations in place, all but five of which had been put in place since 1991, but the constraint on intervention placed on the UN by the sovereign authority of member states had by then led to a situation where international intervention had occurred without seeking UN sanction, most notably in the NATO intervention in Kosovo, and the US-led interventions in Afghanistan and Iraq.

Although some internal conflicts have been contained, many have a tendency to intensify, as has been demonstrated in the wars of the Yugoslav succession (Glenny, 1992; Honig and Both, 1996; Ignatieff, 1994; Lendavi, 1991; Silber and Little, 1996; Thompson, 1992), the Balkans generally (Poulton, 1991), other conflicts such as those in Nagorno-Karabakh (Saroyan, 1990; Walker, 1991), the Kurd Homelands (McDowell,1992), Rwanda (Keane, 1996), Lebanon (Kliot, 1987), other parts of Africa (Harding, 1993), Sri Lanka (Ram, 1989; Spencer, 1990), Fiji (Premdas, 1991), Cambodia (Peang-Meth, 1991), Nigeria (Bach, 1989) and East Europe and the former USSR generally (Goble, 1989; Hatschikjan, 1991). Sollenberg and Wallensteen (2001) pointed out that while most current major armed conflicts are internal, in 14 cases other states had contributed regular troops to one side or the other of the dispute. As these internal conflicts escalated, many displayed a tendency to assume international dimensions. Most ethnic minorities are not confined within a single nation-state: the cases of Serbs in Croatia and Bosnia, Russians within many of the successor states of the USSR, and the Kurds and Chinese in many Asian countries illustrate that ethnic identity often ignores the borders of nation-states. It is not surprising, therefore, that minority groups often look for protection to neighbouring countries or make irridentist claims.

This is not to say that ethnic diversity necessarily leads to divisiveness – to the contrary, ethnic diversity can provide the basis for a vibrant pluralism within which, in the best of possible circumstances, positive interdependence between cultural frameworks is seen to provide the basis for dynamic growth and change. Throughout its history, for example, India took great pride in its pluralist approach to internal ethnic groups based on language, religion, tribes, castes and sects, and arguably, this approach provided a stronger basis for maintaining democratic practice in comparison with religiously homogeneous Pakistan. That said, the rise of Hindu fundamentalism and the decline in the appeal of the Congress Party has seen this pluralistic approach come under threat (Akbar, 1985; Smith, 1991). There has been a conscious effort to celebrate diversity in the US, a process which was encouraged by the Clinton administration's special initiative on race (Berube, 1994; Hawley and Jackson, 1995). Humanity would be diminished if ethnic variety comes to be regarded solely as a divisive and negative force. Indeed, one way this issue can be addressed is to recognise the ubiquity of heterogeneity and the virtue of hybridity (Coulby et al., 1997; Flecha, 1999).

Social theory and ethnicity

As ethnicity has re-emerged as a key dimension in the affairs of states and the relations between states, so too it is possible to trace a new awareness of the importance of ethnic issues within social theory. While social theorists in the nineteenth and early twentieth centuries were interested in conflict in society, mid-twentieth century functionalists neglected conflict in favour of a unitary notion of society and culture which emphasised social integration through common values. When conflict was addressed it was seen as pathological and dysfunctional to the normal operations of society. More recently social conflict has been seen to contain the potential for a positive role in producing the processes and structures of group cohesion through cross-cutting identities. This conceptual reorientation encouraged the development of an empirical base of information on conflicted societies and, with renewed interest in Marxist and Weberian approaches to sociology in the 1970s, saw conflict restored to its place in the centre of social theory and analysis (Darby, 1991).

In another area of social theory, social stratification, there was a recognition of the need to incorporate ethnic stratification alongside more traditional dimensions of investigation such as gender and socio-economic stratification (Parkin, 1979). In a key text in the literature on ethnicity, Glazar and Moynihan (1975) reversed a long tradition within social theory to argue that ethnicity had become the fundamental basis of social stratification in contemporary society, with property now appearing to be derivative (see also, Darby, 1983; Glazar and Young, 1983). By the late 1980s and early 1990s, the literature on ethnic issues and ethnicity was growing considerably (Bacal, 1991; Bracewell, 1991; Caplan and Feffer, 1996; Ignatieff, 1994; Miles and Singer-Kerel, 1991; Rex, 1986; Rex and Mason, 1986; Stavenhagen, 1991). A key feature of this literature has been a break with the 'modernisation' paradigm with its implication that the processes of urbanisation, secularisation and industrialisation would minimise social differences. The process of nation building, it had been believed, would develop modern homogeneous culture centred on patriotic loyalty to the state, rather than on ethnically-based loyalties. The supposed promise of the 'modernisation' paradigm was that 'ascriptive group loyalties would be superseded and would no longer be functional in modern societies', but the promise proved illusory (Bacal, 1991; Esman, 1990; Horowitz, 1990; Ra'anan, 1990; Richmond, 1987).

Research patterns and issues

It is clear, therefore, that ethnic issues have taken on a new importance at national and international levels, and that this is reflected in academic research on ethnicity. Social Anthropologists were among the first social scientists to address issues of ethnicity in studies of isolated and distant cultures (Rex, 1986). Reviewing this literature, Bacal (1991) pointed to four main changes in the uses of ethnicity in anthropology: firstly, he pointed to a shift from the traditional anthropological 'etic' or trait approach to a more subjective 'emic' approach, which suggests a 'psycho-cultural' focus on social belonging and social (ethnic) behaviour. Secondly, Bacal suggested there had been a change from the concern with cultural socialisation in simpler societies to a focus on more complex and multi-national societies. A third feature was the change from the discrete and categorical emphasis within ethnographic approaches, to a relational, dialectical and historical perspective that was concerned more with the dynamics of social inequality. Finally, Bacal pointed to a shift from symmetrical to asymmetrical or conflict perspectives. This shift towards a dynamic conceptualisation of ethnic issues can be seen in other disciplinary approaches.

Social Psychologists have long been interested in the dynamics of prejudice and discrimination (Adorno et al., 1950; Allport, 1954; Bettelheim and Janowitz, 1950), but for the present purposes what was perhaps even more significant was the shift in European Social Psychology towards intergroup research and theory, and a focus on the processes of social identity (Tajfel, 1984), a trend which arguably had not been taken up by North American academic psychologists (Chirot and Seligman, 2001). We explore some these themes in more detail in Chapter 3 of the present volume. The concern with processes of identity was evident also in historical work on nationalism (Hobsbawm, 1990; Smith, 1991). There was a further point of contact between historical, sociological and psychological research on genocide and ethnocide (Bauman, 1989; Chalk and Jonassohn, 1990; Staub, 1989).

Educationalists have long been interested in ethnic and racial issues, both in terms of the participation of ethnic minorities in educational systems and the potential role of education in ameliorating prejudice and discrimination (Berube, 1994; Coulby et al., 1997; Harvard Educational Review, 1988; Hawley and Jackson, 1995; McCarthy, 1991; Phillips, 1991; Pluralism in Education, 1996). While these issues have been most extensively addressed in western states, there has been a broader, comparative interest in education and human rights (Grant, 1988; Kymlicka, 1996; Tarrow, 1987; Modgil et al., 1986). The area of human rights and minority rights has inspired a huge literature with a strong focus on the development of charters and convenants (Davies, 1988). Political scientists have offered ideas on the role of electoral and governmental systems in plural societies (De Guchtenere et al., 1991), while the discipline of International Relations has made an important contribution to issues of governance at national and international levels, and to conflict resolution through mediation (Groom, 1991). In Northern Ireland, Great Britain and North America, academic research has made an important contribution to social policy analysis and evaluation. Further contributions have come from Social Geographers, Urban and Regional Studies, Social Policy Analysis and Social Administration Studies, and the tradition of work derived from Conflict Resolution and Peace Studies (Garcia, 1991).

The key point arising from this is that no single academic or practice tradition lays claim to a focus on ethnicity, nor has as its sole focus research and practice on ethnicity. Rather, ethnicity marks a point at which all of these traditions share a common concern and to which each makes a significant contribution. The notion of ethnicity is, however, replete with terminological and conceptual confusion. There are at least two reasons for this: firstly, at a pragmatic level different interest groups, whether academic or policy-oriented, use different terms to refer to the same issues, or similar terms to refer to different issues. This arises from the situation described above where a plurality of traditions have a shared point of contact on ethnicity.

An additional factor is that discourses on ethnicity can reify socially constructed categories and invest them with an immanent reality they do not deserve. Popular notions of 'race', for example, treat it as a discrete variable based on biological essentialism, whereas in fact there are no discrete 'races' in the human species (Kohn, 1995). A further factor applies more specifically to the conflict resolution tradition where the notion of ethnicity has played a subordinate role because of the macro-level focus of much of the practice within this tradition, and the degree of separation that currently exists between practice and evaluation.

In academic literature, the term ethnicity has been widely used for a relatively short time. In part its use reflected a move away from the language of 'race' because this term carried, and perhaps in popular usage still carries, the pejorative political overtones referred to above. Ethnicity is often understood to refer to some type of cultural distinctiveness. This implies that the idea of an ethnic group only makes sense in a context of ethnic pluralism, or, in other words, an intergroup context. This holds true when the focus on ethnicity switches to primordialist concerns, that is conceptualisations of ethnicity based on fictive lines of descent.

Ethnic identity may be voluntaristic or willed, or imposed, or more usually some combination of both. At a voluntaristic level an ethnic group is a community of people who engage in shared social practices which inform their sense of identity: examples would include religious, linguistic and cultural communities. Bacal (1991) has pointed out that the voluntary dimension of ethnic identity has become more important as a consequence of the democratising forces released by anti-colonial and civil rights struggles of national and ethnic liberation movements in the post-war period. To this might be added the growing literature in post-modernist social theory on the role of new social movements, many of which focus on ethnic or cultural identity as a basis for social mobilisation.

Ethnic identity may be based also on assumed national origins, or on shared phenotypic characteristics such as skin colour. In either case the basis for ethnic affiliation establishes a particular community as distinctive and bounded in some way or other. This distinctiveness should not be seen as unalterable or immutable: people in communities have a multiplicity of available identities and ethnicity only becomes relevant when a particular basis for identity becomes invested with social meaning and significance. This implies that ethnicity, and the notion of an ethnic group, does not exist in any abstract sense, but must be linked to a particular context in space and time: often this context is characterised by a power imbalance between an ethnic minority (or minorities) and an ethnic majority. At a theoretical and conceptual level, therefore, ethnic boundaries are socially constructed and hence malleable, even though in particular contexts they may be treated as timeless and unalterable: in such contexts the ascription of an essentialist character to ethnic identity is usually linked to the maintenance of a power imbalance.

The focus on power imbalance above should not be taken, once again, as an over-concentration on the negative potentiality of ethnicity. It is important to recognise and emphasise the positive, integrating force of ethnicity in contemporary societies. While most, if not all, societies are ethnically plural, not all suffer violent internal conflict between ethnic communities. There is value, in other words, in assessing social policy and practice in societies that have flourished through the celebration of pluralism and diversity.

Constructing divided societies

If it is clear that the role of ethnicity has become more important in national and international affairs, and this is reflected in emerging trends in the academic literature and social theory, how is that divided societies developed? If almost all contemporary states must now be seen as, for all practical purposes, ethnically heterogeneous, even though there are now more independent countries than ever before, what practical processes explain this new imagined reality? Not surprisingly, the historical processes which have created contemporary heterogeneity are prefigured in the discussion above, and it is not difficult to identify some of the basic influences. A simple list of factors might include:

- the impact of colonialism on indigenous peoples;
- the long-term consequences for people forcibly transported from their homelands to other territories;

- the consequences of post-colonial contexts, especially where population movement occurred within a colonial territory for economic
  or other reasons;
- contemporary patterns of economic migration; and
- the continuing cases of territorial disputes.

All these processes have contributed to the development of ethnically
divided societies and all have contributed to the creation of minority
communities in different societies.

European expansion overseas and the seizure of colonies provide one
clear example. In many cases this process of colonialism had deleteri-
ous consequences for indigenous peoples. The most extreme consequences are provided by examples of genocide or ethnocide. Even
when such extreme consequences did not occur, in many colonial contexts the indigenous people were left in the position of an impover-
ished minority, as, for example, in parts of North and South America,
Australia and New Zealand. In some respects apartheid South Africa fits
this pattern, but there the indigenous people had their minority position defined by their political, rather than their numerical, status.

Kolchin (1993) has provided a detailed account of the experience
of slavery in North America, although Giddens (1989) reminds us of
the larger number of Africans that were transported to Central and
South America and of the different experience they had in comparison
to the North. In all cases, the descendants of the slave populations
have remained in significant numbers to contribute to the ethnic
diversity of the societies. Only in rare cases, and for relatively small
numbers, did the descendants of slaves attempt to return physically to
Africa. Liberia is one example where such a return was made, but
ironically, recent internal conflict in that country has some of its roots
in differences between the descendants of indigenous and returnee
populations.

In Africa, a consequence of colonialism has been a very high level of
linguistic and ethnic diversity within post-colonial societies. This is
largely due to the fact that colonial territories were usually demarcated
on administrative grounds, with little consideration for the existing
pattern of settlement. Pre-existent societies were divided or mixed in a
relatively haphazard manner, since the colonisers were little interested
in the views of the peoples whose land they seized. Once independence was achieved in these territories, however, an issue that had to be
addressed was whether or not a territorial rearrangement should
attempt to create a higher degree of internal homogenisation. As we

noted at the beginning of this chapter, the Organisation of African Unity decided that the pursuit of new boundaries was likely to prove, at best, fruitless and, at worst, painful. Better, therefore, to leave the colonial boundaries where they were, and attempt to construct symbols and gain loyalty to the new states. The post-colonial experience has itself been painful and some have questioned the prescience of the Cairo decision (Harding, 1993). But it is doubtful whether an alternative approach, which opened boundaries to question, would have been any more successful: the recent conflicts in the Balkans highlight just how thin the ice of territorial trading can become (Silber and Little, 1996). In the multi-lingual and multi-ethnic societies that were created, however, a basic problem was in determining the language of rule. In practice, in most cases the language of the former colonial power was retained as the language of rule, if only on pragmatic grounds. One effect of this, however, was to contribute to an internal division between western-educated, and sometimes oriented, ruling elites, and the mass of the population. Sometimes this division reinforced that between urban and rural populations. Thus we can see the colonial legacy in the francophone states such as Zaire, the Cote d'Ivoire and the Central African Republic; in the former British territories of Ghana, Nigeria, Zambia and Tanzania; and the former Portuguese territories of Angola, Mozambique and Guinea-Bissau.

A further legacy of colonialism is a result of the movement of populations within colonial territories, often for economic reasons. Thus, for example, within the British Empire there were significant numbers of labourers transported from the Indian sub-continent to other parts of the Empire. The descendants of these economic migrants have largely remained in the post-independence states and contributed to ethnic diversity. In some cases this has led to ethnic tensions at different points in time – examples of this would include South Africa, Trinidad and Tobago, and Malaysia – while in a smaller number of cases it has led to violent ethnic conflict, as in Fiji. This factor is not only historical, however. As we noted above, the collapse of the USSR left significant numbers of Russian-speaking citizens adrift in newly independent states. This was perhaps particularly marked in the Baltic states of Estonia and Latvia: in both cases over a third of the population were ethnic Russian, only small proportions of whom spoke the restored official languages of Estonian and Lettish respectively. A related example was provided by the Soviet Union of Chechens-Ingush and Crimean Tartars in the aftermath of the Second World War. For the Chechens this is remembered as their betrayal by the Soviets and the current generation engages in a bloody war, not only with the Russians, but with other communities who had moved in to replace the deportees in the early 1950s. However, what is perhaps most startling about the Chechen conflict is how the period of relative calm during a large part of the Soviet period looks, in historical retrospect, as but a brief hiatus in a 150-year war (Naimark, 2001).

The importance of economic migration has continued beyond the age of empires. Within Europe there has been significant economic migration from former colonial territories into the metropolitan centres. Countries so affected have included Britain, France, Belgium and the Netherlands. Often economic migrants in these situations were accorded some form of citizenship rights because of the former status of their homelands. This did not, however, prevent the development of prejudice and discrimination as we see in the case of Britain, considered further in Chapter 7. Economic migration occurred within Europe as well and it is possible to identify three main waves. The first largely involved movement of labour from south Europe, including Turkey and Yugoslavia, towards the richer northern states. The second wave involved economic migration from Eastern Europe and the Mediterranean rim. Unlike the first wave, this second wave involved movement into the states of south Europe as well. Unlike the earlier type of economic migration from former colonial territories, these second-wave migrants were normally treated as 'guest-workers', their presence was assumed to be temporary and they rarely were accorded citizen rights. It was noteworthy, for example, that when the Social Democratic government in Germany proposed to accord some citizenship rights to the descendants of long-established 'guest-workers' in 1999 it provoked strong opposition from the conservative parties. In such a situation it was hardly surprising that the minorities are even more vulnerable to prejudice and discrimination.

This has become perhaps even more evident following the third wave of migration into the European Union as refugees flee violence, conflict and intolerance in other parts of the world. A common response in European countries has been to mount barriers to migrants by establishing tough criteria for recognising a right to refugee status and a general disinclination to accept economic criteria as legitimate. In January 1, 2002, there were 19.8 million persons of concern to UNHCR, including 4.9 million in Europe. Of this total, 12 million were refugees, 6.3 million were internally displaced people and others affected by war, and almost a million were asylum seekers. Between 1992 and 2001 an average of 375,000 asylum applications were made to European Union countries and an average of over 150,000 asylum applications to the USA and Canada (source: www.unhcr.ch/statistics)

Another process that highlights the contemporary heterogeneity of states lies in the extent to which state boundaries remain contestable, even if not currently contested. We have alluded to this factor above when we mentioned the contested nature of post-Soviet borders. Within Europe perhaps the clearest example lies in the case of Hungary which lost territory at the end of both World Wars. This had the consequence that a significant proportion of the ethnic Hungarian community lives outside the state in co-terminous state territories. To date this has not been used by unscrupulous politicians as part of a populist irredentism, but tensions are evident in Hungary's relationships with its near neighbours. In the Balkans we have already mentioned the territorial disputes which accompanied the collapse of the former Yugoslavia, but these have not been confined solely to the successor states, as the position of Macedonia shows. At independence the Macedonians found themselves in a potentially unenviable relationship with their immediate neighbours. Bulgaria was content for them to have a state, but questioned their status as a separate ethnic community. By contrast, Serbia was content that they were a separate ethnic community, but prefered them not to have a separate state. Worst of all, Greece denied their existence as a separate ethnic community and lobbied fiercely against their statehood as Macedonia. The implosion of the Milosevic regime in Yugoslavia following the NATO intervention in Kosovo and the internationalisation of that territory appears to have fuelled the ambitions of ethnic Albanians and added an internal pressure to Macedonia's difficulties that broke into violence for a short period.

South of the region we have the continuing partition of Cyprus which is fuelled by, and fuels, the dispute between Greece and Turkey. Territorial disputes in Europe are not confined to the south and east. There are active irridentist movements in a number of countries, although perhaps the most active in recent years has been the one seeking to remove Northern Ireland from the United Kingdom and place it in the Republic of Ireland, albeit now pursued largely through political rather than paramilitary means. The potential for irridentist conflict remains also in South Tyrol. In Spain sections of the Basque community continue to offer support for the groups which would seek to separate the region from the Spanish State, whereas Catalonian separatism appears to have been mitigated to some degree by regional autonomy and de facto federalism in post-Franco Spain. In Corsica a sporadic separatist campaign continues, while in Turkey sections of the Kurdish community continue to pursue the goal of a separate Kurdistan.

In the early part of this chapter we pointed to some of the factors which had helped to restore the contemporary importance of ethnicity and then went on to explore the way in which this interest had been reflected in academic debates and discussions. We then considered briefly some of the material processes that help to explain why the typical condition of modern states is one of ethnic heterogeneity, despite the often-assumed cultural homogeneity of modern nation-states. Even the recent history of humankind has involved an extraordinary level of global movement, whether voluntary or involuntary. As people have moved and settled, so the societies resulting from these processes have come to resemble less the singularity celebrated in the rituals and iconography of the modern 'imagined communities' of the nation–state (Anderson, 1983), but rather a plural mix that contains within itself the seeds of conflict and separation. As societies have moved from an assumed homogeneity to a scarcely avoidable heterogeneity, how have education systems responded to these changes? If, in the past, mass education systems helped to secure the priorities and conditions of mass industrial society (Donald, 1985), how have they responded to current changes? This is the question that provides the basis for the rest of this book.

3
Psychological Perspectives on Prejudice

Introduction

An enduring feature of ethnic conflict lies in the speed with which unimaginable fury can sometimes be raised. It is as if there is a deep well of emotional forces just waiting to be unleashed under propitious circumstances. Whether this is an overly simplistic picture or not, it is perhaps why some people look to psychology for part of the explanation for ethnic conflict. This chapter will examine some of the general themes that emerge from psychological work on prejudice by focusing on a number of key moments in research and theorising. The first part of the chapter will examine the way in which psychologists examined people's methods for perceiving and making sense of the world, including their consideration of some of the cognitive processes involved in perception, such as categorisation and stereotyping. The next main section of the chapter will examine two of the main theories of prejudice that have developed within social psychology, based on research in the US in the 1950s, and in Europe in the 1980s. In the final part of the chapter we will examine some of the themes to emerge from a later body of work where some psychologists have focused on the role of language in the social construction of reality. To close the chapter we will briefly point to some of the implications that arise from the discussion as a whole. The reason for examining these themes from social psychology is the potential insight they provide to the inter-relationships between people, particularly those which seem to foment prejudice and discrimination. All too often these are characteristics of divided societies.

Perception

An important theme in psychological work on the way people perceive the world is to recognise that we do not simply receive stimuli in a passive and uninvolved way. Rather, people actively try to understand and make sense of the world. Many psychologists suggest that this active process of perception differs between people who adopt different 'thinking' styles. Thus, for example, a 'reasoned thinker' would be someone who considered a variety of bits of evidence before drawing conclusions about some phenomena that had been encountered. By contrast, a 'prejudiced thinker' would be someone whose prejudice can influence the weight they attach to different bits of evidence. In other words, the 'prejudiced thinker' is likely to place more weight and importance on evidence that supports his or her prior position. The difference between thinking styles and its link to perception can be perhaps best seen in the work of Adorno et al. (1950) on the concept of the Authoritarian Personality and was used by some to try to offer some element of explanation for the horrors of the Holocaust.

More generally, psychologists typically describe three general cognitive processes as playing a role in perception: selection, accentuation and interpretation. The idea of selection implies that we all choose from the perceptual evidence available at any point in time. This is simply because of the sheer volume of information we can conceivably draw on. Once we have selected from amongst the available perceptual information, we tend to place excessive weight on the value of that which has been selected. In other words, we accentuate or exaggerate the importance of this information. We then base our interpretation or understanding of what we are seeing on that evidence. We all select, accentuate and interpret, but what is said to differentiate prejudiced thinkers, in comparison to reasoned thinkers, is that they tend to follow each of these processes in a more exaggerated way. Thus, prejudiced people are more likely to seek simple explanations and are more likely to attribute causes to people, or groups of people.

A corollary of the process of selection is that of categorisation. One way of dealing with the sheer volume of perceptual information we encounter is to categorise aspects of the world into explanatory clusters. By categorising in this way we simplify perceptual information and render it easier to cope with: to live in a world where we treat each new stimulus as unique and different would be to live in an increasingly complex and confusing world, so categorisation has a value in providing some degree of control and stability in our experience.

Psychologists describe two types of categories, differentiated and monopolistic categories. Differentiated categories are those that are flexible, towards which people are prepared to be critical and which are amenable to change as new information is encountered. By contrast, monopolistic categories are rigid and fixed, and are more likely to be defended than changed in the face of conflicting evidence. Not surprisingly, given these definitions, reasoned thinkers are considered to make more use of differentiated categories, while prejudiced thinkers are more likely to make use of monopolistic categories. In either case the type of category fits with the attributed cognitive style.

If this is so, then why do we not all simply use differentiated categories? If we remember that the point of categorisation is to simplify the world in order that we are better able to understand and hence deal with it, then we can see the value of monopolistic categories in that they offer a more certain account of part of the perceptual world. On the other hand, a plethora of differentiated categories may produce confusion and uncertainty given their nature. To inhabit either end of this continuum then has clear disadvantages, but the question then arises as to whether or not there is some happy medium.

Stereotyping

A particular form of categorisation lies in the process of stereotyping. A stereotype refers to a set of beliefs about a category of people. Normally when we refer to stereotyped views of a group of people we usually imply that the stereotype involves negative beliefs. Stereotyping can, however, just as easily refer to a positive image of a group of people. In either case, the stereotype usually implies certain expectations about the behaviour of the category of people and they often provide the basis for justifying particular action towards members of the category. A negative stereotype, for example, can be used to justify treating members of the group badly or unfairly, whereas a positive stereotype can be used to justify favourable treatment towards members of that group.

There was a time when some psychologists had argued that in order to be socially effective, that is to say convincing, stereotypes had to be based on a 'kernel of truth'. In other words, at its heart the stereotype would have to be based on some element of fact that appeared to be entirely true, even when a significantly larger framework of beliefs and perceptions that may not be true was built upon this base. More recent views have placed less weight on the need for a 'kernel of truth' and somewhat more on the functional consequences of stereotypes. In this vein a stereotype is described as affecting the process of selection in that it is likely to lead to an easy acceptance of evidence that confirms the stereotype, and a rejection of evidence which appears to contradict the stereotype.

What we can see in this account, therefore, is that people actively try to understand the world. In doing this they categorise the information they perceive, in order that the sheer volume of information can be dealt with better, and judgements and interpretations are based on this simplified version of the perceptual world. One example of these processes is that we categorise people. This can lead to the development of generalised stereotypes of particular groups of people, and these stereotypes can, in turn, affect the way in which we deal with new perceptual information.

Having outlined some of the general themes from the way psychologists have attempted to understand cognitive processes involved in perception and the ways in which these can affect our perception of people, we will next look at two key theoretical frameworks which have developed from social psychology. Both attempt to understand how the types of cognitive processes we have described above are translated into prejudice and discrimination against groups of people.

The Robber's Cave studies

During the 1950s a series of field studies were carried out by Muzafer Sherif and his co-workers in an attempt to understand the processes that lead to prejudice and intergroup conflict (Sherif et al., 1961; Sherif, 1966). Summer camps run in Robber's Cave provided the basic model for their studies. In a typical field study they took two groups of boys to a summer camp and kept them separate for the first week or so. During this time they noticed the development of a group identity within each group of boys. After a period of separation, the two groups of boys were brought together in a series of sporting and other competitions. Meeting in this way was found to very quickly produce intergroup conflict between the boys, above and beyond the organised competitions. Having created a situation of intergroup conflict so easily, the researchers then began the process of trying to reduce the conflict.

The first strategy they used was based on bringing the boys together in non-competitive situations, that is to say, a contact strategy. To their chagrin, however, not only did these contact episodes fail to reduce conflict between the two groups, but rather they were used by the boys as opportunities to get at the other group. Contact alone, in other words, tended to escalate the conflict still further. The researchers were able to identify one type of contact that did go some way to reducing intergroup conflict. This involved the use of superordinate goals, that is, goals which both groups wanted to achieve, but which neither could achieve independently. In fact most of the superordinate goals in the study had to be specially organised by the researchers to occur 'spontaneously' and their positive impact only became evident over a number of specific instances. One example of a superordinate goal was when the boys were told that the truck carrying the food for the evening meal had driven off the road into a ditch. The only way anyone was going to eat that evening was if both groups worked together to haul the truck back onto the road. The researchers found that after a series of these 'fortuitous accidents' the level of conflict between the two groups of boys did start to reduce and they began to show evidence of treating each other in an unprejudiced and reasonable manner.

Sherif argued that the field studies had highlighted the theoretical importance of interdependence in understanding group behaviour. Competitive interdependence was seen to lead to intergroup hostility and conflict, while cooperative interdependence was seen to lead to a reduction of hostility and more peaceable intergroup relations. He went on to argue that this had some resonance for the wider world where, for example, the Cold War between the USA and the USSR was following the track of competitive interdependence. For this reason he felt that the conflict was likely to escalate over time. By contrast, he argued that the two superpowers could be put back on a more peaceful track if they identified and worked together on some superordinate goal. The goals he suggested lay in medical or space research. One can see the potential relevance for this explanation for any intergroup situation where the groups perceive themselves as being in competition for scarce or limited resources. In a situation where the groups see a gain for one side as necessarily a loss for the other, then the relationship between the groups will very quickly become one of competitive interdependence, with all the negative consequences implied by Sherif's research findings. In other words, Sherif's work suggests that when two groups see themselves as competing over a scarce resource, or as being involved in a zero-sum game, then there are likely to be added psychological pressures that will exacerbate the perceived conflict and make it harder to contain. However, in an important comment on this explanation, Billig (1976) has pointed out that the superordinate goals in the Sherif studies only appeared to be spontaneous occurrences, but were in fact arranged by the third group in the study, the researchers. It is not always immediately evident from where an analogous *deus ex machina* will emerge when groups within a society find themselves in a situation of competitive interdependence.

Sherif's work had demonstrated the importance of a social dimension in psychological theory and practice, but in the 1960s there was hardly any research based on the social dimension. There was, however, a lot of research and theorising based on the psychology of the individual, although in truth this may simply have been the reassertion of the individualist tradition that had been established in academic psychology by the victory of the behaviourists in the 1930s. Thus, for example, the behaviour of dissident groups was explained by such approaches as the frustration-aggression hypothesis, which suggested that a combination of internal and external circumstances could trigger an aggressive response on the part of an individual. This instinctual, non-rational prescription carries with it a clear political judgement that decries these acts of resistance. This is even clear when we note that, at the same time, conflict between elites was more typically examined through the lens of game theory, that is, the idea that people in conflict acted as 'behavioural accountants' in the rational pursuit of ends. Both sets of explanations were rooted in the psychology of the individual, rather than the psychology of the group (Billig, 1976) and, despite the claim to objective neutrality, carried within themselves implicit political judgements on which forms of violence were legitimised or de-legitimised.

Social identity theory

One social psychologist who tried to return to the social dimension was Henri Tajfel. He had an interest in the role of categorisation because of a very simple experiment he had carried out in the 1960s (Tajfel, 1981). In this experiment two groups of subjects looked at a drawing of six lines and were asked to estimate the difference between each of the lines. In one situation the six lines were presented simply as six lines. In another situation the three shorter lines were labelled as 'group A', while the three longer lines were labelled as 'group B'. In other words, the only difference between the two situations was that in one of them the perceptual stimuli were categorised. Tajfel found that the estimates in the situation where the lines were categorised tended to understate the differences within the groups, and to overstate the difference between the groups. The fact of categorisation, in other words, seemed to be sufficient to influence people's perceptions. If this could happen for judgements about the length of lines, reasoned Tajfel, could it happen also for judgements about people? In a series of experimental and other studies from the 1970s onwards, an accumulating body of evidence suggested that this was indeed the case.

In a typical study subjects for an experiment would arrive at a test centre and carry out a fairly mundane task: in some of the early studies (Tajfel et al., 1971) they were asked to estimate the number of dots on a series of slides, or to indicate how much they liked each in a series of abstract paintings. Following this task, subjects would be told, individually, that the pattern of results allowed participants to be categorised into one of two groups: under- or over-estimators, in the case of the dots, or those with a preference for Klee or Kandinsky, in the case of the paintings. They were then asked to complete a further booklet as part of a second experiment. Each page in this booklet contained a series of number pairs, each one of which could be assigned to a member of their group or a member of the other group. The instructions for the subjects informed them that they had to choose one pair of numbers on each page, effectively awarding points to anonymous members of the two groups in the study. They were told also that the points would be totalled up for each participant at the end of the study and converted into a monetary value. The situation that was therefore achieved was one where all the normal features of an intergroup context, save the fact of categorisation, were removed. Participants in the study knew they were a member of a group, and that unknown others in the study were members of this group also. However, there was no face-no-face interaction between group members, the groups had no history and, beyond the confines of the study, they had no future.

Two key findings emerged from the study. First, participants tended to show favouritism towards members of their own group by awarding them maximum points where possible. However, there was an important caveat to this behaviour: the pattern of favouritism towards ingroup members was shown only where this did not offer any greater advantage to outgroup members. Thus, in a situation where awarding maximum points to an ingroup member would involve awarding even more points to an outgroup member, participants typically preferred to award less in absolute terms to an ingroup member, as long as this meant the ingroup member was awarded more than an outgroup member. Their goal appeared to be one of maximising the difference between the groups, in favour of their own group. In other words, whereas the first finding indicated a pattern of favouritism towards the ingroup, the second finding indicated a pattern of active discrimination against outgroups members (Tajfel, 1970; Tajfel et al., 1971). In the context of the experiment the participants seemed not to be interested in the collective good, or of the abstract good of their own group, but rather their priority seemed to be to win.

In later versions of the experimental paradigm participants were categorised into the groups on the toss of a coin. However, the general pattern of results was maintained: when people were categorised into two groups, even on an overtly random, trivial or transient basis, then they behaved in a way which favoured members of their own group and discriminated against members of the other group. When the mechanism for demonstrating this behaviour, through the awarding of points on the number pairs, was changed so that their monetary value was removed, that is, they were simply described as 'points', the discriminatory behaviour was actually enhanced.

The main approach that developed from this work was termed 'social identity theory'. In essence this argued that part of our identity is based on the social groups to which we belong. In an echo of Said's (1978) argument on 'orientalism', social identity theory suggested that we base our sense of social identity not only on the characteristics of our own group, but through comparisons between our group and other groups. Furthermore, it argued that, because we want to maintain a sense of positive self-esteem, we make these comparisons on dimensions that cast our own group in a positive light. This is not necessarily a destructive process. If gross stereotypes can be excused in order to illustrate the point, it may be that the French favourably compare themselves with the Germans on the basis of style and culture, while the Germans favourably compare themselves with the French on the basis of industry and efficiency. In other words, intergroup social comparisons can lead to favourable outcomes for both groups if they compare themselves on different criteria and do so in a context where the structure of relationship between them is not mediated by competition over scarce resources.

The problem arises when social comparisons between two groups do not allow for a positive evaluation of the group, when this outcome is seen by at least one of the groups to be unfair and when the context of relations between the groups is seen to be amenable to change. Thus, for example, in Northern Ireland the nationalist minority may have always resented its minority status and the way the group was treated by the unionist majority, but despite that fact that social comparisons between the nationalist and unionist communities may not have afforded a positive contribution to self-esteem for members of the nationalist group, no action was taken to change the situation because it was not seen to be changeable. Thus, it took a particular set of circumstances (in this case the collapse of the authority of the civil authorities and police in the face of widespread rioting) before the minority community felt that anything could be done to change the situation in which it found itself. Furthermore, it is conceivable that the nationalists' sense that their subordinate status was illegitimate may have been fuelled by the fact that they formed a majority on the island of Ireland and that the division of the island itself was seen to be unjust. The corollary, of course, applies. Unionists' sense of self-assurance, and the self-perceived legitimacy of their position, will have been heightened by the fact that they formed the majority within Northern Ireland. However, this may have been tempered by a sense of insecurity due to their minority status on the island of Ireland, which in turn may have motivated an approach which maintained distance and difference between the two communities in Northern Ireland. The nation-state system is a mechanism that claimed to allow for the stable and secure expression of identity on the basis of internal homogeneity. Situations such as Northern Ireland appeared to represent the awkward interstices and fault-lines left over from the territorial settlements that followed the end of the two World Wars in Europe (Gallagher, 1996), since the pursuit of territorial homogeneity seems doomed to inevitable failure. Social identity theory offered some insights on the psychological consequences that flowed from these situations.

The example of Northern Ireland highlights another, more general, aspect of social identity theory. Tajfel (1981) argued that the consequence of group membership contributing negatively to self-esteem was different for dominant and subordinate groups. For dominant groups one reaction might be to accept the illegitimacy of its position and promote change. More usually, he suggested, dominant groups would seek to reassert justifications of the status quo, or create new justifications on why change should not occur. For dominated groups, on the other hand, a wider range of strategies is theoretically available. At an individual level, some members of the dominated group may seek to cross over between the groups, or leave the situation altogether. Alternatively, the dominated group may attempt to assimilate, *in toto*, into the dominant group. In practice, of course, there are often social and material factors that deter or prevent such strategies of crossing, whether by individuals or groups. In situations where crossing or exit is neither desirable or possible, a dominated group is likely either to attempt to change the social evaluation of their group's distinctive characteristics, or alternatively, to change radically the context of relations between the groups. These can be seen as strategies of reform or revolution respectively.

Ideology and discourse

Thus far we have commented on three moments in the psychological work on prejudice and intergroup conflict. One aspect that seems to be missing from the discussion so far is any role for agency, that is the ability of people themselves to affect the flow of events. This may be a problem in many psychological theories, perhaps because many psychologists spend so much time watching people doing things in experiments, and so little time asking them why they did these things. In the present context the concern that arises from a lack of agency is the implication that the psychological processes and forces we have described are completely beyond our influence. More particularly, if the psychological processes which encourage prejudice and intergroup conflict are conceptually no different from the normal processes we use to make sense of the world, might we not descend into a fatalistic conclusion that prejudice and intergroup conflict are inevitable parts of the human condition?

This is not to posit a naïve rationalism or to claim that we exercise complete control over our fate. Social theories in the late nineteenth and early twentieth centuries challenged the rational assumptions of enlightenment thinking and confronted humankind with a less comfortable world. Marx argued that the economic forces of society drove it inexorably from one class formation to another; Durkheim sought to uncover the unspoken rules and rituals that bound people into communities; while Freud dug deep into the mind to try and understand the psychical battle that waged below the conscious level, but which profoundly influenced behaviour. The point is not whether any of these theoretical formulations were accurate or not, but rather that they prefigured a view of the world in which a variety of forces, be they social, economic or psychic, could affect behaviour without anyone being immediately aware of their influence. Nevertheless, the enlightenment does provide us with some basis of optimism in that people do make choices and can consciously aspire to better ways of being. We may not be fully in control, but neither are we hapless puppets.

An attempt to provide a less avowedly, or potentially, deterministic account can be seen in the work of social psychologists on discourse and ideology (Billig, 1976; 1985; see also, Billig, 1987; Potter and Wetherell, 1987). This conceptualisation of ideology eschews the traditional separation of attitudes, beliefs and values and the dissociation of individual attitudes for the purposes of quantification. By contrast, Billig argues that an ideology represents a framework of ideas shared by a social group, that this framework is socially constructed through action in the world and that these ideas can be made real, or take on an appearance of permanence, through institutional or symbolic features of the world. Since the construction of ideology is related to practice and practice is mediated by power, Billig (1976) suggests that the notion of 'false consciousness' be recognised, that is, the notion that an ideology may not accurately reflect the interests of a particular group. Of course, as Billig points out, to label an ideology as a 'false consciousness' is itself an ideological decision. Additionally, over-indulgent use of the concept can displace more detailed consideration: for example, traditional Marxists could 'explain' the lack of revolutionary zeal among West European workers as due to 'false consciousness', when in fact all that was done was to recast the terms of the problem.

This social conceptualisation of ideology can be further refined by Gramsci's differentiation between 'organic' and 'arbitrary' ideologies (Hoare and Smith, 1971). The former are 'necessary to a given structure' in that 'they *organise* human masses and create the terrain on which men move, acquire consciousness of their position, etc.'. Arbitrary ideologies, on the other hand, are 'rationalistic or willed... (T)hey only create individual *movements*, polemics and so on ...'. If we consider the case of Britain, the liberal-democratic ideas that are institutionalised in the parliamentary system may be considered as part of the organic ideology which seems to have a relatively high degree of consensual legitimacy or acceptance, while conservatism, liberalism or socialism are all arbitrary ideologies.

Differentiating between organic and arbitrary ideologies highlights the ideological pluralism of social groups: a subordinate group will not permanently acquiesce in its subordinate position, so we must allow for the possibility of the development of a revolutionary ideology. The source may be within the social group in what might be termed as ideological subgroups. Whereas the ideological framework of the wider social group may be thought of as the consensual shared norms and values of the group (organic ideology), the ideological subgroups would present more particular accounts (arbitrary ideology). The latter element might present a particular definition of the group, a detailed interpretative account of the ingroup's past or a variety of strategic programs which they feel the wider group should adopt. Consider the example of Britain: if we define the British people as a social group then the British political parties could be considered as ideological subgroups within that wider social group. Building on this notion of ideology, Potter and Wetherell (1987) have shown how language is used actively to construct and justify particular versions of reality and ascription of meaning. What we have, in other words, is a view of discourse that suggests that we socially construct the worlds we live in through the material processes involved in language and practice. This is not an enlightenment view of autonomous individuals freely constructing their own worlds, but recognises the press of past generations through the invented, but nevertheless socially effective, weight of tradition. These are social constructions in that they arise from communities of people and serve as a shared set of assumptions for organising social living. Children are socialised into these shared assumptions, but may challenge them as they grow older and come to create their own versions of understanding. The assumptions are, in any case, dynamic and open to change, but are probably robust under normal circumstances.

Conclusion

In this chapter we have considered some of the broad themes which have informed psychological discussions on prejudice and intergroup conflict over a considerable period of time. We focused on a number of particular moments in the development of psychological theory. In the early, pre-war, years, psychologists sought to understand some of the basic processes involved in perception and how, if at all, they might influence the development of prejudice within some people. One of the main themes to emerge from this work was that while there might be some differences in the ways prejudiced and tolerant individuals use cognitive processes, they all used essentially the same type of processes. Later research by Sherif and Tajfel highlighted the relative ease with which intergroup behaviour, and even conflict, could be generated. These could be contrasted with the relative difficulty in finding mechanisms for reducing conflict once it had occurred. In general, however, a similar emergent theme came from these studies as with the earlier ones: the processes involved in conflict and prejudice appear not only to be common, but also to be completely normal. This might lead to a fatalistic conclusion that, if categorisation is inevitable, then the division of people into separate groups is inevitable, and so too is inter-group conflict. It is almost as if there is a danger that we get caught in the inexorable drift of cognitive and other processes that are beyond our control. While it may be true that conflict is easier to start than to prevent, and easier to prevent than to stop once it has started, the work on discourse and ideology reminds us of the importance of human agency, however constrained. We, each of us, inhabit particular universes of meaning, and share many aspects of those universes with other like-minded people. Inevitably, others will provide some dimensions of those universes of meaning to us, but we actively engage with our subjective worlds, and face the option of choices at key moments. Conflict may be the most likely relationship between groups in close proximity, and it is certainly ubiquitous, but the idea of agency and the mechanism of social construction through discourse suggest that conflict is not inevitable. But any explanation which places human agency close to the core necessarily raises the issue of how particular discourses are presented, maintained and changed. And it is here that the role of schools potentially comes into play.

4
Structural Solutions: European Experiences

Introduction

In Chapter 2 we examined the way in which the issue of ethnic division has reasserted its importance. This reassertion occurred despite the assumption of modernisation theory that traditional bases of identity would wither in the face of modern technology and communication, and be replaced by 'more relevant', utilitarian criteria. Of course, as we also saw in Chapter 2, it is not difficult to identify social divisions within most societies albeit the key lies in the consequences of those divisions for social practice. Historically the most common way in which states have responded to the reality of internal social divisions is to emphasise the essential unity of society or play down internal differences in the face of fundamental differences with external others. From a Durkheimian perspective, this goal can be pursued through the establishment of central institutions of governance, and the promulgation of common rituals and practices towards iconic images of the state and nation. Alternatively, states may recognise societal diversity and offer some legitimacy to this through some form of decentralised institutions, albeit within limits. There is a number of particularly interesting examples of such structural diversity within Europe and it is to these that we turn in this chapter. The main aim of the chapter is to examine the consequences for education systems within such decentralised arrangements. Before examining our case studies we will first examine briefly intra-societal divisions within western European states.

Social cleavages

The very notion of Europe arguably arose from a perception of difference, in particular the struggle between Christian Europe and Islam (Said, 1978). Islamic domination of territory to the east and south of Europe, including Spain, up to the fifteenth century, helped to establish the territorial boundaries of the European continent and cast its character as a Christian continent. Indeed, it may not have been until the threat from Islam appeared to recede that European Christianity had the luxury of turning in on itself with the Reformation and subsequent wars of religion in the sixteenth and seventeenth centuries. As Lane and Ersson (1994) pointed out, the religious cleavages established at that time persist in contemporary societies, even though most contemporary societies have gone through processes of secularisation which make religious divisions somewhat less prominent than they once were. They point to three broad categories of societies:

- the largely Protestant countries of northern Europe, especially Scandinavia;
- the largely Catholic countries of southern Europe; and
- the group of countries in between which present a heterogeneous religious structure.

This last group includes countries such as the Netherlands, Switzerland, and Germany and, to a slightly lesser extent, Great Britain. Across all of these countries, Lane and Ersson suggest, the religious fragmentation of Europe has remained almost unchanged, but almost all have experienced processes of secularisation.

At a broader level of generality, Lane and Ersson examine ethnic cleavages in western European states. They focus their definition of ethnic affiliation on language, or the presence of a perceived common culture based on language within a community of people. On this basis they devise a series of 'ethnic fragmentation indices' as a measure of the importance of ethnic cleavages within societies. Their data highlight the three most ethnically diverse western European states as Belgium, Switzerland and Spain. In Belgium the two main ethnic communities are the Dutch (or Flemish)-speaking Flemings, and the French-speaking Walloons. The Flemings comprise about three-fifths of the population while the Walloons comprise about two-fifths. In addition, there is a small minority of German speakers. Lane and Ersson present data that question the extent of national identification in

Belgium, in that whereas 41 per cent identified themselves as Belgian, 58 per cent identified themselves with their linguistic community. This was particularly evident among the Flemings where a community identity was preferred by 67 per cent (see Lane and Ersson, 1994, Table 2.20, p. 83).

In Switzerland the predominant ethnic community is comprised of German speakers. Thereafter the main language communities are French and Italian speakers, with a small proportion of Romansch speakers and a variety of other language groups comprised of 'guest-workers' who do not hold Swiss citizenship. In some parts of Switzerland linguistic differentiation is overlaid by religion, as between Protestant and Catholic communities. In comparison with Belgium, however, Lane and Ersson suggest that national identification is some-what stronger in Switzerland. Thus, for example, a clear majority of German speakers identity themselves as Swiss. While the proportion who prefer this identity among Romansch language speakers is lower, at 40 per cent, they do as a group identify with the Swiss nation more than with any alternative (see Lane and Ersson, 1994, Table 2.21, p. 84).

The third case highlighted by Lane and Ersson is Spain. Almost three-quarters of the Spanish population speak Spanish, or Castellian, as their first language, but there is a number of active minority languages, including Catalan, Basque and Galician, which have a territorial specificity. Indeed, it is the territorial specificity that is most interesting in the Spanish example. Lane and Ersson show that in most parts of the country there is a fairly unambiguous identification with the Spanish nation. There are, however, a number of areas with a significant, if minority, level of regional identification, and a small number of areas where regional identification is at least as strong as identification with the central state.

For the present purposes these examples are interesting not only because of the extent to which their societies contain ethnic divisions based on traditional, that is, more long-standing, criteria, but also because they represent perhaps the best examples of western European states that have developed federal political structures. The main example of a federal state not included here is Germany, but the reason for the adoption of a federal structure after the Second World War was more to do with the experience of the Nazi state and, in particular, the desire to ensure that state structures were not so centralised that a danger existed of state power being abused by extremist political leaders. In each of the three cases we have highlighted above, that is

Belgium, Switzerland and Spain, the establishment of federal political institutions has led to a degree of decentralisation in responsibility for education matters.

The key point of interest lies in the social and political consequences of this decentralisation, in particular the decentralisation of education. If mass education systems in most modern states serve, at least in part, to promote a sense of common identity throughout society, then what role is played by the education system when it is run by local, as opposed to central, authorities? One of the possible consequences of structural decentralisation is to enhance particular identities, but normally this is permitted in order to reduce centrifugal forces that might encourage separatism and thus to maintain the overall unity of the state. The federal 'deal' is often that minority identities are legitimised and the fear of assimilation is removed on the one hand, and the integrity of the state is accepted on the other hand. In this way it is hoped that any separatist pressure will dissipate. However, this strategy runs the potential risk of enhancing division and separation as structural autonomy becomes reinforced over time through the institutions of the regions. There is a necessary tension between the regional and central authorities in a federal state, and these tensions might be exacerbated if they reinforce an existent basis for identity, such as language, religion or nationality. The three cases to be examined in this chapter combine high levels of political decentralisation and ethnic divisions. In the discussion we will explore the consequences of the former on the latter and its impact on educational policy and practice. In each country we outline the history of relationships between the diverse communities in a little more detail and consider the structural arrangements for education within their federal political systems. We then examine the consequences for educational practice in each case.

Switzerland

As discussed above, the major language communities define ethnic diversity in Switzerland: a little under two-thirds of the population speak German as their first language, a little under one-fifth speak French, seven per cent speak Italian and about one per cent speak Romansch. In addition, some ten per cent of the population, but not the citizenry, are made up of other ethnic identities, such as Spanish, Portuguese, and Turkish, mainly as 'guest-workers'.

Switzerland is organised into a confederation of twenty cantons and six half-cantons. Beneath the cantonal level lie some 3,000 communes that range in size from 20 to 250,000 people. The decentralised nature of the system is emphasised by a commitment to the procedures of direct democracy in which referendums are used regularly to make decisions. In this way, many decisions have to be taken at the level of the commune first, then at the level of the canton, and only then, if at all, at the confederal level (OECD, 1991: p. 56). A federal tribunal, comprised of thirty judges appointed for six-year terms, has final jurisdiction in disputes between cantons and the confederal authorities, and between cantons. In addition, each canton has its own system of justice, including civil, criminal and appeal courts.

The decentralised nature of the state was embodied in the 1848 and 1874 constitutions, and subsequent amendments. Under Article 3 of the constitution responsibility not otherwise defined as belonging at the confederal level automatically falls within the responsibility of the canton. The constitution also provided for free, compulsory education. Under the 1874 constitution the responsibility of the confederal government was restricted to higher education. The cantons were required to establish elementary schools for which they received subsidies from the confederal government, but the latter exercised no power as a result of the subsidies. The elementary schools teach pupils in the language of the canton, but the other national languages can be studied as well (Kallen and Sauthier, 1995).

The decentralised nature of the state is such that the central government has little to say on education as this is within the competence of the cantons, and, as if to emphasise the point, there is no federal ministry of education. An attempt was made to pass a constitutional amendment in 1973 to give more power to the central state in educational matters. Although this was accepted by a small majority of voters, the smallest possible majority of cantons rejected it:

> This failure shows that the cantons are very anxious to safeguard their almost exclusive authority in educational matters. Therefore, there is no Swiss system of education: there are 26 cantonal systems. (Gretler, 1995: p. 948).

Each canton has its own school law and department of education, and considers its authority in this area as a marker of its distinct identity (OECD, 1991: p. 175; Allemann-Ghiondas, 1994). Not surprisingly, however, different cantons have developed different practices with regard to education. At secondary level, some cantons have largely comprehensive systems, while others have differentiated tracks through secondary education. Some cantons have elected consultative bodies on educational matters. In some, further decentralisation takes place into districts, with elected local educational authorities. In all cantons an inspector supervises teachers, but in some cantons these are part-time fellow teachers, while in others the inspectors are full-time staff of the department of education. The end result, according to Gretler, is a series of multilevel systems that are very close to the populations they serve, but within which the rate of change is very slow because important decisions are voted on by the population.

The slow rate of change is well illustrated by Hega (2001) in a consideration of debates over second language teaching. The problem arose due to disputes between the cantons on the preferred second language to be taught in primary schools. Language teaching has always been an issue in Swiss schools, especially in bilingual or multilingual cantons. The coordinating body for education across the cantons (see below) agreed in 1975 that the first foreign language in schools should be one of the four official languages of Switzerland. The important consequence of this was that English could not be given prior status in second language teaching. However, as Hega (2001) points out, by 1990 only nine of the cantons had implemented the recommendations, although 14 others had ratified legislation for implementation. The remaining three cantons, all of which are German-speaking and border on other predominantly German-speaking cantons, had not passed any legislation on this issue. The reason for the delay, Hega argues, is due to the interplay of community, canton and state interests.

Currently the educational role specified for the confederal government is as follows: it oversees vocational training, regulates gymnastics and sports, runs various federal institutions and grant systems, and supports scientific research and special education. Beyond these specified measures educational responsibility is decentralised. We have noted above the diversity in practice between the cantons, but is there any basis for coordination across the cantons? As early as 1897 a conference of cantonal directors of education was established to exchange information and experience, and to provide a basis for coordination at the national level. Despite this mechanism, however, the cantonal systems remained quite separate up the Second World War. Concerns about harmonisation increased in the post-war period, and particularly from the 1960s onwards.

In 1970 a concordat was agreed between the cantons 'to develop the school and harmonise their respective cantonal legislation' (OECD,

1991: p. 176). The need for referendum support for the detailed measures in the concordat meant that the process took 15 years to complete. Even so, one canton has not signed the concordat, but operates within, and contributes to the financing, of the agreed framework. The resultant agreement covers the starting age and period for compulsory education, and the length and starting point of the school year. In addition, the concordat offers the basis for harmonisation on a range of other issues including reforms, recognition of diplomas, and co-operation on research planning and educational statistics. Other inter-cantonal agreements cover issues such as the funding of joint institutions and access to schools outside cantonal boundaries. There are particular agreements, for example, between cantons that have an affinity for geographical, historical, and perhaps most importantly, linguistic reasons. At a general level, however, the most important agreement lies in a 1979 accord on the funding of universities.

Under this agreement, non-university cantons agreed to pay contributions to cantons with universities. The *quid pro quo* was that students from these non-university cantons received the same rights as 'home' students in university cantons. For the present purposes, the key point of relevance is that despite the fact that a high level of administrative and legal decentralisation created the possibility that coordination across a diverse set of educational systems would become difficult, if not impossible, in practice a reasonably high degree of harmonisation has been maintained. This has occurred because of a perceived common interest in a relatively narrow range of concerns, including inter-cantonal mobility. If these parts of the systems were to mesh, however, a wider extent of harmonisation had to cascade down the system. The infrastructural arrangements for these agreements themselves have extended the range of possible areas of agreement, albeit within a torturously slow decision-making procedure. In this example, in other words, decentralisation has not led to fragmentation since there remained a common practical interest on some level of mutuality between the decentralised education systems. This outcome is not so evident in our next example.

Belgium

The two main ethnic communities in Belgium are the Flemings and Walloons, and they are distinguished by language. There is also a smaller, German-speaking community in the eastern part of the country. The Flemings, who are of Germanic origin, speak Flemish (Dutch), while the Walloons speak French. The predominantly Flemish provinces, in the region called Flanders, are in the north of the country. Brussels is a bilingual enclave within Flanders. These three regions became official federal regions in 1993. About 60 per cent of the population live in Flanders, a little under one-fifth live in Wallonia and about ten per cent live in Brussels.

General educational developments mirrored closely the pattern in other European countries, with its own particular features. Thus, in the 1950s there was a great deal of controversy and political division on the issue of the funding of Catholic schools. The dispute led to the collapse of one government and the establishment of an unlikely (for Belgium at the time) coalition of Liberals and Socialists. This coalition came up with a solution which, however, was rejected at the next election. Following the election a national school committee was established comprising the presidents of the three main parties, and they managed to agree a compromise, the Schools Pact, which was set to run for twelve years. After this time the Pact was renewed and the issue has never seriously resurfaced in Belgian politics (Fitzmaurice, 1996: p. 47; Vanderstraeten, 2002).

This did have a wider significance, as it was only one of a series of issues that were increasing pressure towards some form of decentralisation. Fitzmaurice (1996) divides the subsequent reforms of the state towards federalism into four main phases: between 1970–1979, 1980–1987, 1987–1991, and the present. The point at which the step away from the unitary state began was in the recognition of linguistic frontiers in 1963. The first attempt to provide a new legal framework for Belgium was in the 1971 constitution and subsequent legislation that provided for four states within a federation. The states were to be Flanders, Wallonia, Brussels and the German-speaking areas, each of which would have autonomous powers over a range of cultural and socio-economic matters. As a bilingual area, however, Brussels was unable to exercise responsibility over the cultural domain, while, according to Fitzmaurice, the arrangement for the German-speaking areas was anomalous, as they did not have a common socio-economic interest. Attempts to solve the anomalies created by this wholly territorial solution to the problem were followed over the next decade.

In the second stage an attempt was made to separate the territorial and cultural dimensions. Thus, the solution at this stage was based on the establishment of three councils for the Dutch, French and German-speaking communities, and three regional authorities for Flanders, Wallonia and Brussels. The communities were to have responsibility for 'personal' matters, including hospitals, welfare services, vocational training, language, and local aspects of education and international cultural cooperation. The regions had elected councils with, in the case of Brussels, a built-in protection that censure motions, and elections to the executive had to have a majority in both linguistic groups.

As on the previous occasion, the years following the agreement saw the passage, or attempted passage, of legislation designed to fill in the fine detail. By the end of the decade this solution too had failed to provide a workable basis for the country and so another solution was sought. An agreement was reached between the main political parties and it included such provisions as the full communitarianisation of education, the devolution of additional powers to the regions and the extension of the powers of the communities and regions in international affairs. In other words, the states in the federation moved even further apart. Once again, however, agreeing a plan for a coalition government proved easier than implementing all parts of the plan. In fact, the government fell in 1991 with the final elements, ironically dealing largely with the competences of the central government, still to be finalised.

The final, formal step towards separation followed the 1992 *Accord de la St Michel* and the 1993 constitution that declared Belgium to be a federal state. Under the constitution the number of elected representatives in the institutions of central government was dramatically scaled back. Effective power was placed in the hands of regional governments and the community councils. The community councils were given responsibility for education.

We can see in this brief overview of Belgian political developments how social polarisation was addressed through policies that led to greater institutional separation as part of a seemingly inexorable drive towards federalism. The effects of this can be seen quite clearly in education. In the early 1960s there were two ministers within a single Ministry of Education. By the early 1970s this had changed to a situation where the Ministry itself was split in two for the main linguistic communities. Towards the end of the 1980s the German-speaking community joined this split by establishing its own Ministry of Education. The formal move towards a federal state has further institutionalised this process.

Verhoeven (1992) has provided some insights into the consequences of this increasing division. He examined the way in which the separate educational authorities for the three communities dealt with a range of educational issues, including the rights of teachers, the quality and inspection of education, local school administration and arrangements for the education of the children of migrants. With the exception of the final area, Verhoeven found that the policies adopted in the three communities were diverging quite rapidly, even though the formal step towards federalism had only occurred quite recently. In large part this has resulted because the separation has not been combined with any mechanism for coordination or contact between the authorities. The federalisation of education has, in other words, further separated the three communities. In the field of education this separation and divergence has occurred so quickly that it is difficult to see how the systems could be linked together, even if the will to do so existed. This example provides a contrast with Switzerland in that Belgium appears to be a state that has unravelled over the years due to political de-centralisation. In the particular area of education there are now three separate systems and they are moving further apart.

Spain

The second Spanish Republic followed the election of a coalition of left-wing parties in 1931. The coalition gave autonomy to Catalonia and extended the principle of home rule to the Basque Provinces in the north. Land reform measures were introduced, education was secu-larised, the Jesuit order was dissolved and Church-state ties were ended. In 1933 a coalition of centre-right parties was elected and began to reverse some of these measures. Left-wing and regionalist groups opposed this retrenchment, leading to social instability, the collapse of the coalition in 1935 and the election of a new, left-wing coalition in 1936. This coalition restored the previous measures, but social instabil-ity remained high. In July 1936, groups of military officers attempted a take-over. They achieved a measure of success in the south, but were rapidly defeated in the north. The resulting division provided the battle-line for a bloody civil war that, in some ways, provided a precur-sor for the Second World War. The civil war ended in April 1939, with the defeat of the government forces and the establishment of a military dictatorship under General Franco.

The brutal nature of the war, the vindictive peace that followed and Franco's sympathy for the Axis during the Second World War, all con-tributed to the isolation of Spain until, in the mid-1950s and in the context of the Cold War, external relations with some western coun-tries thawed. Within the country, improved economic conditions were accompanied by a degree of liberalisation, albeit within a centralist and unitary conception of the Spanish state that gave no recognition to the claims of regionalist groups for some autonomy. The most notable effect of this pressure was in the cycle of violence between the illegal Basque paramilitary group, ETA, and Spanish security forces between 1969 and 1975. Although other regionalist interests existed, most notably in Catalonia and Galicia, violence in these areas was much more sporadic than in the Basque territory.

Franco died in 1975 at which point Juan Carlos, who favoured a transition to democracy, was crowned King of Spain. Political parties were legalised and in 1977 a centre-right government was elected following free elections. In 1978 the Spanish parliament passed a new constitution which provided for a constitutional monarchy, freedom for political parties, and autonomy for the historic nationalities of the Basques, Catalans and Galicians, and accorded similar rights to the regions. Seventeen autonomous communities were recognised in the constitution, with the Basque Provinces, Catalonia and Galicia being allowed to take the lead in the pursuit of home rule and indigenous language rights as recognition of their status as 'historic communities'. In 1981 there was a change in Prime Minister and an attempted coup by the military and civil guards. The coup was defeated, as was another planned effort in 1982, just before elections in which PSOE, the Socialist party, was decisively elected to government. The process of regionalisation continued. The constitution allowed for progress towards autonomy to proceed at different speeds and, as noted above, it was in the three historic communities where the most rapid changes took place precisely because these were the areas where the greatest pressure for secession existed (Herrez, 1995). These regions were to be closely followed by Andalucia, the Canary Islands and Valencia, so that by the mid-1980s autonomy had been extended to six regions. The process was slower in the remaining regions as they had to develop the basis of regional identities (Hanson, 2000). Not surprisingly, political considerations arising from coalition governments at times hastened or slowed the process. Thus, in the mid-1990s the Socialist government required the support of Catalan and Basque nationalist parties to survive and, in return, offered even greater regional autonomy and benefits. After the 1996 election the new right-wing government also required the support of Catalan nationalists in order to remain in power, a fact which limited its ability to reverse some of the curriculum initiatives that had been started under the Socialists (Hanson, 2000).

In education the central state retains responsibility for the general organisation of the school system, the regulations for obtaining, issuing and validating degrees and certificates, and the operation of a central inspectorate. All other areas of education may be transferred to the responsibility of the autonomous communities. In this way the federalisation of education is based on a common central core.

> Educational administration in Spain is consequently an administrative instrument of the state or of the autonomous communities, according to the distribution of responsibilities which exist in each case. The political and administrative system of the Spanish state must guarantee the unity of the education system, which may be provided and administered in each autonomous community with different educational programmes, priorities and objectives, provided that these observe the minimum requirements established in state legislation governing the validation of degrees and certificates and the essential unity of the system. (Herrez, 1995: p. 107).

An issue of key significance to some of the autonomous communities lies in the role of language. While the new constitution describes the national character of the state and declares that Spanish, or Castillian, is the official state language which all citizens have the right to use and the duty to know, the other languages of Spain are recognised as official within their respective autonomous communities. As Boyd-Barrett (1995) suggests, this recognition seeks to realise the promise of the constitution that 'the distinct language traditions of Spain represent a cultural heritage which will be the object of special respect and protection' (Boyd-Barrett, 1995: p. 208). Although the constitution does not explicitly allow teaching in community languages, the consensus has been that such a practice is implied. In any case, in Catalonia, Valencia, Galicia and the Basque territories there have been progressive moves towards increased community language teaching in schools (see, for example, Ferrer, 2000, for a discussion on the situation in Catalonia). Thus, in most areas of Spain the central Ministry of Education regulates about two-thirds of the curriculum, with the remainder regulated by the autonomous community. Within autonomous communities with their own language, the balance of responsibility for regulation of the curriculum falls to 55 per cent for the central Ministry and 45 per cent for the community (Herrez, 1995).

In Belgium the move towards federalism accompanied the deterioration in relations between the communities and, as we have seen above, has widened the separation between them. In contrast, in Spain the move towards federalism was designed to aid the process of reconciliation between communities, some of whom had been involved in violent conflict with the central state. Something of this feeling can be found in Esteve's (1992) discussion of the role of education in Spain and the wider lessons he draws from this experience for the developing European Union. Esteve highlights the continued existence of regional identities, often based on language and culture, throughout Spanish history and despite active attempts to impose a unitary cultural identity throughout society. This 'melting-pot' strategy of assimilation was pursued with particular vigour during the Franco regime when minority languages were actively suppressed. In democratic Spain, by contrast, the rights of the communities have been recognised and legitimised, and, as we have seen above, this has had a particular resonance in education policy. Esteve suggests that this represents a move away from an assimilationist, melting-pot strategy, towards a new model based on the celebration of diversity.

> ... the politics of the melting-pot have been replaced by the politics of the salad bowl in which the different ingredients are mixed, with the idea that each one confers its distinctive flavour to a pleasing and harmonious whole whose distinctive character is determined by the nature and diversity of its components (Esteve, 1992: p. 261).

Esteve goes on to suggest that the positive aspects of the approach to education in Spain should inform the development of the European Union. Quite apart from the political and institutional links which this system encourages, which themselves will raise educational demands and priorities, the European Union is marked also by the freedom of movement among its peoples. Increased mobility is likely to lead to more diverse classrooms and challenge the insularity of curricular content, materials and books. The priority, for Esteve, is to find a way of developing an awareness of European unity while at the same time conserving not only the identities of the member states of the Union, but also of the component regions and minorities within those states. The model he offers is the Spanish experience where an attempt is being made to build unity through the recognition and celebration of diversity.

Esteve was writing at a point when the full effects of decentralisation had yet to be felt and his analysis is tinged with as much hope as anything else. On one level, however, Hanson's (2000) analysis suggests that Esteve's hope has been realised. Hanson argues that while decentralisation took twice as long as planned, it nevertheless did result in a radical, and in many ways extraordinary, break with the centralist practice of the Franco era. Also, in all but one region a consequence of decentralisation appears to have been a reduction in separatist pressures. Only in the Basque Provinces is there still violent opposition to the political settlement, although the level of support for the ETA campaign appears to be small. Thus, decentralisation has not produced the fragmentation of the state. However, Hanson concludes with a cautious note as he questions the strength of the various mechanisms which have been introduced to ensure that all the communities operate within parameters set by the centre. Now that autonomy has been achieved, he suggests, the next test will lie in the operation of these centralising mechanisms. Another caveat is provided by Aguado and Malik (2001) who question whether the attachment to diversity actually extends to newly arrived migrants in Spain.

Conclusion

We began this chapter by considering evidence on the role of social cleavages in western European states. The three states with the highest level of internal ethnic fragmentation were Belgium, Switzerland and Spain. These three states are interesting in another respect in that all have developed federal political systems. In the case of Switzerland the federal polity is of long standing and is combined with an elaborate system of direct democracy that has the consequence of further decentralising the operation of power and decision-making. In Belgium the federal institutions represent the latest attempt to devise political structures acceptable to both main language communities and follow a series of innovations from the 1960s onwards. In democratic Spain the federal arrangements, and in particular the granting of the right of autonomy to regional communities, are of even more recent origin. These changes have occurred quite rapidly in the aftermath of, and in reaction to, the centralist policies of the old regime. In each of the three cases education policy has been devolved to some degree as part of the federal arrangements, although as the case study discussions have shown, the implications in each case have been quite different.

There has been relatively little threat to the territorial integrity of Switzerland. The high level of decentralisation has provided a basis for holding the diverse country together. The level of decentralisation is such that it would have been quite possible for the different cantons to go their own ways on key areas of policy, including education. However, there was a pragmatic recognition of the value of maintaining some points of contact between the education systems in each of the cantons, even if only so that some degree of mobility could be maintained at the tertiary level. In order to maintain these points of contact, however, it has been necessary to pursue a somewhat higher level of harmonisation between the systems in order that a practical basis for tertiary level mobility can operate. The situation in Belgium could not provide a starker contrast. There, as a consequence of the evolving separation in the institutional relationship between the main communities, the links in education have become ever more tenuous. In Switzerland people talk of 26 education systems, not one, but this is belied by the active attempts to maintain harmony. In Belgium people talk of two education systems and the division is more profound. With few, if any, remaining links between the two main systems, the policymakers in each area have taken their school systems in different directions to the extent that any attempt to reverse the situation and restore some degree of harmony would be replete with difficulty. Again the contrast with Spain is striking. In Belgium increased levels of autonomy have been granted in order to reduce conflict, but at the cost of greater separation. In Spain the decision to grant autonomy was seen as a logical recognition of the intra-societal diversity that had been denied, and often brutally suppressed, during the Franco regime. In the context of a democratic Spain, decentralisation, both institutionally and, for some regions, linguistically, was offered as the best way to hold the country together and neutralise the centrifugal separatist pressures that had existed in various regions. In the discussion above we got some sense of the positive hope that is invested by some Spanish educationalists in this model and the successes that have been achieved so far.

Overall, and in the context of our present interest, perhaps the most interesting conclusion to derive from this examination of three case studies is that it raises questions about purely structural educational solutions to ethnic problems. In the case of these decentralised states, the implications for educational policy and practice has been quite different. In one, a limited set of contacts provides the basis and incentive for greater harmony. In another decentralisation has led to rapid separation, while in yet another decentralisation is seen as the historic compromise that will mitigate separatist pressures. Structural solutions, in other words, contain less than predictable consequences, and depend on their own specific context. This unpredictability of outcomes should serve only to emphasise the difficulties involved in trying to mitigate ethnic tensions through educational solutions. If only life was so simple.

5
Civil War to Civil Rights

Introduction

A general area of interest in relation to the role of education includes societies that are coping with the arrival of new ethnic communities. In these cases the traditional priority has been in trying to find ways of assimilating the new communities into the host community. A slightly different set of issues face 'migration societies' where the majority is comprised of inward migrants or their descendants. In this case the priority often revolves around some form of 'melting-pot' within which diverse peoples can be moulded into a new common identity. Perhaps the best example of the 'melting-pot' approach can be found in the USA and it is to features of this example that we turn over the next two chapters. This chapter will examine the general features of policy in relation to ethnic diversity up to the mid-1960s and largely address issues around the segregation and desegregation of schools. The next chapter will examine the debates and disputes following the mid-1960s which were marked mainly by disputes over busing and other anti-segregation measures, and the continuing debate over affirmative action.

Government in the US

In order to understand political change in the US it is useful to be aware of the particularities of its political system as laid out in the US constitution. The framers of the constitution saw themselves as the standard bearers of liberalism, a radical philosophy at a time when the rights of free citizens were being cast in opposition to monarchical rule. This was the time when the US, and later France, was beginning to demonstrate that a state could exist without a King at its head. In keeping with their liberal ideology the framers of the constitution attempted to find a balance between the two, potentially competing, principles of 'equality' and 'freedom'. The principle of equality implied the need for a strong central authority in order to ensure that conditions of equity were maintained among citizens. On the other hand, the principle of 'liberty' implied the need for a weak central authority in order to minimise the danger of tyrannical government. Opposition to arbitrary government was, after all, one of the reasons why the US came into being. In practice the way in which these potentially competing concerns were resolved was to build a series of 'checks and balances' in the political system.

The checks and balances in the system can be seen in three main areas. First, political power was decentralised by the establishment of a federal system of government. Under this system a central federal government was established, but with clearly defined roles and responsibilities (and limits). Alongside the federal government, however, was the decentralisation of significant powers and responsibilities to the individual states that made up the federation, and even to city authorities. Under the constitution the main responsibility of the federal government at the centre was to promote the defence and welfare of the community. The constitution does not accord the federal government any defined role in education. As we will see below, this constrained the ability of Presidents to push through changes in the education system. Responsibility for education was firmly located at the state and local levels. In practice, however, the main way in which the federal government tried to legitimise its role in education was through its responsibility for ensuring equality.

A second basis for maintaining a check and balance in the system of government lay in the 'separation of powers'. In order to limit the danger that government might abuse its power or exceed its authority, a clear division was created between the different functions. Thus, legislative responsibility was given to the two houses of Congress, and they were to be elected under different mechanisms to reflect population and geography across the country. Executive responsibility was vested in the President who could propose legislation, but in order to be enacted it required the support of Congress. The third element of the separation of powers lay with the Judiciary which was responsible for defining the applicability of specific laws. The written constitution provided the basis upon which the entire edifice was constructed, and the final arbiter on the meaning and definition of the constitution was vested in the highest court, the Supreme Court. From a practical point of view this arrangement was of crucial significance. If the legislature was unsympathetic to reforms on 'race' issues and the President was insufficiently motivated to press the issue, the Supreme Court provided an alternative route for campaigners if it was possible to argue for a more radical understanding of key clauses. In practice this was one of the main routes used to advance the cause of greater racial equality in the US and takes us to the third basis for maintaining checks and balances in the system (Tindall and Shi, 1999).

The third check on the abuse of political power lay in the fact that the core principles defining the relationship between state and society were written down. In relation to equity perhaps the best known statement lies in the opening phrases of the Declaration of Independence, 1776:

> ...We hold these truths to be self-evident, that all men are created equal; that they are endowed by their Creator with certain inalienable rights; that among these, are life, liberty and the pursuit of happiness. ...

Of course, as Lee (1988) has pointed out, such phrases are susceptible to different interpretations. In the particular case of the US it proved to be possible to hold to a 'self-evident' belief in equality while maintaining a system of slavery. Thus, for example, the number of members of the House of Representatives was determined by the population of each State, but the constitution had to provide a basis for counting the population and, in particular, the slave population of states. The relevant section of the constitution (Article 1, Section 2, subsection 3) stated that the population would be determined by:

> ... the whole number of free persons, including those bound to service for a term of years, and excluding Indians not taxed, three-fifths of other persons.

Slaves, in other words, were legally to be considered as less than a complete person. The Supreme Court ruling in Dred Scot vs Sandford 1857, confirmed the lesser status of slaves by ruling that, as they were not citizens, they were not entitled to the constitutional protection accorded to citizens. The key significance of this ruling was that it was determined as applying anywhere in the country, including States that had outlawed slavery.

The constitutional clause establishing slaves as 'three-fifths' of a person was removed by the 14th Amendment, one of a series of amendments passed during the post-Civil War Reconstruction period, as we shall see below. For the present the importance of this amendment lies in its promulgation of the principle of 'equal protection of the law', as this was the basis upon which many later attempts at progressive reform were based:

> Section 1: ...No State shall make or enforce any law which shall abridge the privileges or immunities of citizens of the US ... nor shall any State deprive any person of life, liberty, or property, without due process of law ... nor deny to any person within its jurisdiction the equal protection of the law.

But before the passage of this amendment there was the Civil War.

The Civil War and its aftermath

The Civil War, 1861–1865, was a defining moment for the US. One in twelve adult American males fought in the war and more were to die than in the Second World War almost a century later. Indeed, since the Civil War it was not until the terrible events of September 11, 2001, that there was to be as great a loss of life in a violent incident in a single day in the continental USA. For the African-American community, however, the most important consequence of the Civil War was in the nationwide abolition of slavery. More than this, however, the period following the war that came to be known as 'Reconstruction' marked an opportunity for African-Americans potentially to enjoy the fruits of citizenship. It marked also a period, albeit transient, when the potential for freedom and equality was explored.

In the immediate aftermath of the war some of the States of the former confederacy passed a series of 'Black Codes' that virtually restored many of the restrictions of the slave regime. In reaction to this Congress in Washington denied seats to all members from the eleven Confederate states and established a Joint Committee on Reconstruction with members drawn from the Senate and House of Representatives. The group within the Republican Party that led these initiatives came to be known as the Radicals. African–Americans in the South, too, contributed to the new dispensation by establishing Churches and schools, restoring families, and through the exercise of the franchise, electing over 600 of their number, most of whom were former slaves, as State legislators. The reaction from White Southerners was swift. As early as 1866 groups, such as the Ku Klux Klan, were established to terrorise African-Americans and Radical political leaders. Ironically, in the same year the Radicals in Congress were able to secure the passage of a Civil Rights Act. Over the same period the 13th, 14th and 15th Amendments to the Constitution were passed and approved, as were a series of Reconstruction Acts which attempted to lay down a legal basis for equality.

It was not to last. The reaction against Reconstruction was swift. Widespread intimidation was used to reverse the post-war political gains achieved by African-Americans and restore the old interests in the seats of government of Confederacy states. President Johnson, who had replaced the assassinated Lincoln, was unsympathetic to the Reconstruction cause and tried to block Radical legislation. In response the Radicals made an unsuccessful attempt to impeach him. In a short time, however, war weariness in the North, allied with increasing concerns in other areas, undermined Radical attempts to press the case for racial justice in the South. This combination of terror within and distraction without played into the hands of Southern conservatives. By 1870 all of the former Confederate States had been readmitted to the Union and by 1877 all had seen the re-establishment of conservative rule (Tindall and Shi, 1999; Franklin, 1994). Once the old regimes had been restored, in fact if not in name, the newly constituted State governments began the process of obviating civil liberties laws and passing segregationist measures in what came to be known as the 'Jim Crow' laws. In essence the 'Jim Crow' laws sought to restrict access to voting rights by Blacks and to encourage segregation in as many areas of social life as possible. Inevitably many the measures adopted in this period were going to be tested before the Supreme Court. In the event, a position of stability was to be established before century's end.

An indication of what this new stability was to entail came with the Supreme Court ruling on the legality of the 1875 Civil Rights Act as this was predicated on a conservative reading of the constitution. The 1875 Act sought to outlaw discrimination and segregation, but was declared void by the Supreme Court following a series of civil rights cases considered in 1883. Under this ruling the Court declared that the 14th Amendment applied to States, but could not be applied to individuals. On this basis the Court decided that the Civil Rights Act was *ultra vires* the power of legislature as it had no basis for constraining the behaviour of individuals. This interpretation permitted the maintenance of segregationist laws that required the provision of separate facilities for African-Americans and Whites. The specific legality of these measures was tested in the case of Plessy vs. Ferguson,

1896, which was to set the context for race relations in the US for a generation.

The case itself arose from a dispute over separate facilities for White and Black passengers in trains in New Orleans. The argument before the Court depended on whether or not enforced separate facilities could be justified under the constitution. The Court ruled that the provision of separate facilities for different races was consistent with the constitution if they met the standard of being 'separate but equal'. This provided a green light for those who wanted to pass segregationist laws which now came aplenty and informed not just the provision of services, but also social conventions (Polenberg, 1980: p. 25; Tindall and Shi, 1999: pp. 853–854). This was particularly marked in education. By the 1950s 17 of the 21 southern states, and Washington DC, had legally enforced segregated schools, all justified on the basis of the 'separate but equal' ruling. Thus was the final nail driven into the brief flowering of equality measures during Reconstruction. From this point, agitators for civil rights had to choose an incrementalist strategy in an attempt to chip away at the basis of 'separate but equal'. In particular, they decided to avoid a direct challenge to the Plessy ruling until such time as a challenge had a high probability of success. This was the strategy adopted by the National Association for the Advancement of Colored People (NAACP), founded in 1910, when it sought to restore the weight of the Reconstruction Amendments by targeted legal challenges to discriminatory actions.

In education the NAACP decided to focus its attention at two levels. First, it targeted higher education rather than schools, in part because the lesser provision of higher education institutions made it easier to avoid circumstances where parallel facilities existed and some basis for a 'separate but equal' provision could be argued. Second, it focused, where possible, on Law Schools. The tactical ground for this decision was that Supreme Court Justices were more likely to be sympathetic to the value of education in these institutions. On this basis, then, began a series of challenges that, over time, were, slowly but surely, to undermine the foundations of the Plessy ruling. What follows is a brief account of some of the more significant cases.

The Missouri ex rel. Gaines vs Canada 1938, case dealt with a situation where an African-American applicant had been refused admission to an all-White college despite the fact that there was no alternative all-Black college available within the State. The plaintiff had been offered an out-of-State alternative and it was on this basis that the State authorities were trying to claim 'separate but equal' provision.

However, the Court ruled in the plaintiff's favour and established the principle that the 'separate but equal' criterion had to be operable within state. A further progressive gain was made in McLaurin vs. Oklahoma State Regents 1950. In this case an African-American applicant was accepted to a State university, but was obliged by the university authorities to use separate facilities from White students. The authorities were trying to maintain segregated arrangements by adopting internal segregation and arguing that the fact of being permitted to attend the institution provided the basis for equality. However, once again the Court ruled in favour of the plaintiff. This time the Court's decision was on the grounds that the requirement to use separate facilities, in this instance, impaired the ability of the African-American student to complete his course.

Despite these decisions, the creative imagination of those wishing to hold back change remained unbounded. In Texas an attempt was made to create an entirely new Law School, with a tiny handful of students and Faculty, rather than admit an African-American applicant to the Texas Law School. In Sweatt vs. Painter 1950, the Court ruled that this could not be deemed as providing an equal option and so was also illegal. Once again, the Court ruled that the African-American applicant should be accepted to the college. All three cases were important in that they set limits on the extent of the 'separate but equal' principle and provided the basis upon which a direct challenge to the Plessy ruling could be made. That opportunity came with Brown vs. Board of Education 1954.

The 1954 ruling arose from the consolidation of a series of cases from four States and was debated and considered over several years before a decision was rendered (Raffel, 1998: pp. 31–36). The core issue concerned the legality of laws which required children to attend separate schools at a time when, as the Court determined, the role of public education had changed considerably in comparison with the end of the previous century. The Chief Justice found himself coming to the view that the only remaining justification for legal segregation was a belief in the inherent inferiority of Blacks and this was not a belief to which he could adhere. Given this, he set about writing a decision that would reflect the landmark status of the Court's ruling while maintaining unanimity among the Justices. The key section from the Court's ruling has been widely quoted, but bears repeating here:

> To separate some children from others of similar age and qualifications solely because of their race generates feeling of inferiority ... Separate

facilities are inherently unequal. ... Therefore we hold that the plaintiffs ... are ... deprived of the equal protection of the laws guaranteed by the 14th Amendment.

As with the Plessy decision in 1896, the Brown decision marked a key moment in the evolution of race relations policy in the US. It overturned the 'separate but equal' principle and thus removed the legal basis for enforced segregation, but required further discussion on action to be taken across different circumstances. This led to a second ruling, Brown II 1955, in which the Court decided that school district authorities had the primary responsibility for assessing and solving these problems and that District Courts had authority to oversee the exercise of this responsibility. The Brown II ruling went on to state that desegregation should be seen as a requirement, not an aspiration, and moves in this direction should be taken 'with all deliberate speed'. However, despite the use of a phrase which implied urgency, the Court did not offer specific recommendations on a timetable for desegregation. This aspect of the ruling has been criticised for not setting time limits on the achievement of desegregation and not providing clear guidelines on implementation. For both reasons it left an opening for excuses for delay. Raffel (1998: pp. 35–36) goes on to suggest that these lacunae might have been less due to oversight and more due to a pragmatic realisation by the Court of the difficulty of implementing any measures of desegregation in the South at all.

Pursuing civil rights

Despite this problem, an immediate consequence of the Brown ruling was to provide a firmer basis for activist attempts to overturn segregationist laws across a range of services. One opportunity was seized when Rosa Parks refused to give up her bus seat to a White passenger, as required by City ordinances, in Montgomery, Alabama (Garrow, 1993). The bus driver had Rosa Parks arrested, but the response of the African-American community was to boycott the buses. Not only did this put the issue of civil rights on the front pages of US newspapers, but also it brought to public attention a young pastor who was to become an iconic figure in the struggle for civil rights, Martin Luther King Jr. The Montgomery bus boycott helped to encourage action by a reluctant Eisenhower administration, in particular through the passage of the Civil Rights Act in 1957. During its legislative process parts of this Act were removed so that it was eventually reduced to dealing largely with voting rights. But, while the law was weak and was pursued by Eisenhower's Department of Justice 'with all deliberate lethargy' (Schlesinger, 1978: p. 308), it nevertheless marked another important step along the path:

> Too emasculated to register a tangible impact in southern polling booths, the bill, as the first civil rights measure to pass in eighty-two years, nevertheless marked a significant milestone. (Polenberg, 1980: p. 160).

Further pressure was provided by the extraordinary spectacle created when Governor Faubus of Arkansas called out the National Guard to prevent the enrolment of nine African-American children in the Central High School, Little Rock, Arkansas. Once again a reluctant Eisenhower was obliged to take some action, this time sending Federal troops to deal with this affront to the Supreme Court ruling. The City's response was to close all its schools in 1958, and attempt, unsuccessfully, to privatise Central High School and hence take it out of the ambit of the Brown ruling. While perhaps the most publicised case, this was only one of a number of examples across the South where attempts were made to resist the implications of the Brown ruling.

In the same year less notice was taken of a situation in another part of the country. In the post-Second World War period William Levitt saw an opportunity to meet the nascent demand for inexpensive suburban housing . His first development, christened Levittown, comprised more than 17,000 homes in Long Island in the late 1940s. Another Levittown of 16,000 homes was built in Pennsylvania, followed by another of 6,200 homes in New Jersey. In 1957, of the 60,000 people who lived in Levittown, Pennsylvania, not one was African-American. The first African-American family to move in was greeted with hostility and two months of active harassment that only ended after a court order and a promise by the governor that violators of the order would be punished. It was not for another three years, however, that Levitt himself agreed to allow Black families to move into the developments:

> Levitt screened Black purchasers to ensure they were solidly middle-class ... and he dispersed black families across the development so that no two ever occupied adjacent homes. Wherever possible, he arranged for [Black families] to buy the last house on the street ... so as to reduce their visibility. ... In June 1960, thirteen years after the

first white family had bought a house in a Levittown office, the first black family bought one. (Polenberg, 1980: p. 163).

Perhaps the main significance of this series of events lay in the way it emphasised the problem of segregation in Northern states. In the South, where 'Jim Crow' laws mandated segregation in many spheres of life, attempts to overturn the laws themselves provided a basis for beginning to redress segregation. In the North, on the other hand, segregation was a *de facto* condition, rather than a *de jure* one, thus making it harder to attack directly. Meanwhile, the Civil Rights movement, having been boosted by its success in Montgomery, continued to step up its activity.

In the 1960s four Black students in Greensboro, North Carolina, sat at a Whites-only lunch counter and refused to leave. In 1961 James Farmer and others led 'Freedom Riders' into Southern states in an attempt to desegregate interstate bus terminals (and *inter alia* encourage the intervention of Federal authorities), only to meet the solid opposition of the White citizens and the police. In 1962 James Meredith enrolled in the University of Mississippi only for the situation to develop into a reprise of Little Rock. This occurred again the next year when the Governor of Alabama, George Wallace, vowed to prevent the integration of the University of Alabama. However, bit by bit, the efforts to implement the Brown decision to desegregate began to bear fruit.

The efforts were aided by an increasingly proactive President Kennedy, even though his administration adopted a fairly pragmatic approach to the achievement of morally conceived goals. Thus, for example, when the Civil Rights movement called a march on Washington in 1963, the initial reaction of the administration was to try to persuade the organisers to cancel the march. When this did not work, the administration sought agreement with the organisers to moderate the tone of the speeches and convert its main orientation away from a protest against federal inaction towards a demonstration of support for the Civil Rights bill which was then before the House. The bill itself was pursued through active negotiations with the Republican minority in the House.

The Civil Rights Act was passed in 1964 and contained measures to outlaw racial discrimination in the provision of a wide range of goods and services and employment. It empowered the Attorney-General to eliminate segregation in public property, including schools, libraries, museums, hospitals and playgrounds. And it allowed for the withholding of public funds from federally-assisted projects that failed to desegregate (Polenberg, 1980: p. 190).

Although there had been hope that this and other measures would have removed barriers to Blacks' voting, in practice restrictions were still practised in some Southern states. For this reason the Voting Rights Act was passed in 1965 in order to end the use of literacy tests and authorise the use of federal registers to enrol voters. As Polenberg (1980) pointed out, this measure had a dramatic effect in some of the Southern states. Thus, for example, African-American voter registration rose from 19 to 61 per cent in Alabama, from 7 to 67 per cent in Mississippi, and from 27 to 60 per cent in Georgia.

As the situation seemed to be improving in the South, however, the situation in the North was taking a more violent turn. The rhetoric of civil rights, allied with the legal measures, increased expectations on the extent of progressive change. In the African-American ghettos of the Northern cities, resentment simmered and grew, and began to break out in riots that spread from place to place. There was serious rioting in New York in 1964, Los Angeles in 1965 and Detroit in 1967. Coincident with these developments was the growth of a more radical position within African-American communities that placed less emphasis on integration and more emphasis on the espousal of a new Black pride (X, 1966). Arguably, the move of some towards a new separatism and Black nationalism was reinforced by the political radicalisation engendered by increasing US involvement in Vietnam. The radicalisation and rioting increased even more after the assassination of Martin Luther King in 1968. An inquiry into the riots, which we will examine in more detail below, highlighted the role of prejudice, segregation and racism in fomenting the conditions for violence, and the fact that relationships between African-American communities and White police were poor and deteriorating (Kerner Commission, 1968: pp. 203–5).

As a response to the civil disorder, President Johnson established the Kerner Commission to investigate the background and reasons for the riots and to offer suggestions for new policy initiatives to quell the problem. For present purposes the Kerner Commission report is of particular significance as it provided a clear and studied insight into the comparative condition of schooling in the Northern cities and, in particular, into the Black experience of schooling. The Commission offered conclusions and recommendations on a wide variety of areas, but in education it concentrated on three main issues: segregation in schools, comparative patterns of resources, both human and material, in different types of schools, and the nature of school-community relationships.

The Commission concluded that a high level of *de facto* racial segregation operated in Northern schools. Three-quarters of African-American children were in schools with more than 90 per cent African-American enrolment, while over 80 per cent of White children were in schools with more than 90 per cent White enrolment. This segregation had material consequences: the teachers in the majority African-American schools were generally less well qualified than their peers in majority White schools. The majority African-American schools were more likely to be over-crowded, the buildings were older and the schools were generally less well-equipped than majority White schools. This comparative pattern was linked to the location of majority African-American schools in inner-city areas. These schools received less money due to a declining or stagnant tax-base in many inner-city areas. In addition, these schools generally had more non-school demands, related to upkeep and maintenance, on their funds. Finally, the Commission concluded that the relationships between majority African-American schools and their neighbourhoods were poor: the pupils' parents were often suspicious and hostile towards school authorities, and few of the teachers in the schools lived in the neighbourhoods of the schools.

Following these conclusions, the Commission recommended four basic education strategies to be pursued. First, since segregation and isolation lay behind so many of the social problems between the races, including attitudinal, social and economic issues, the Commission recommended that school integration was vital to the future of the country. Second, despite the priority of pursuing integration in schools, the Commission accepted that schools in inner-city areas were likely to remain dominated by children from disadvantaged minorities for the immediate future. In these circumstances integration was unlikely to be possible, but it was important that these children did not suffer additional disadvantage. Thus, the Commission recommended that the quality of inner-city schools should be improved dramatically and that 'equality of results with all-white schools in terms of achievement should be the goal' (Kerner Commission, 1968: p. 439). The Commission did not see this recommendation as in conflict with the goal of integration. Among the findings of the report was the suggestion that even in integrated schools, ability tracking often created situations where racial segregation occurred within schools. Thus, compensatory education in the short-term would, it was hoped, contribute to wider integration in the longer term. The third recommendation was that active attempts should be made to build links and confidence between inner-city schools and the communities they served. Finally, in order to enhance the relevance and aspirations of minority children the Commission recommended an expansion of opportunities for higher education and for vocational training.

The Commission went on to suggest some specific measures that might be pursued towards the achievement of these goals. These included the provision of additional aid to school systems seeking to desegregate, attempts to attract dedicated new teachers to work in inner-city schools or to provide all-year education for disadvantaged pupils. They went on to suggest other initiatives such as special measures to support early years education, extra incentives for highly-qualified teachers to work in inner-city schools, a reduction in max-imum class sizes, wider recognition of diverse communities and traditions in school textbooks, greater concentration on basic skills and the provision of additional services for severely disadvantaged or dis-turbed pupils. Even this brief résumé of the Commission's conclusions indicates the scope and range of its recommendations. At the time of its publication it provided the basis for a policy agenda with obvious links to President Johnson's Great Society programme.

The retrospective view on the Kerner Commission's recommenda-tions has, however, been mixed. Thernstrom and Thernstrom (1997) criticised the Kerner Commission on the basis that its recommend-ations were based on a snapshot picture of a situation that had, in their view, changed considerably over the preceding years. Thus, Thernstrom and Thernstrom argue that the employment prospects and experience of African-Americans had been steadily improving by the time Kerner reported, but that this dynamic had not been taken into account. The Great Society push for reform, which was to embrace the controversial issue of affirmative action, was, in their view, largely unnecessary as the problem was solving itself already. However, despite the mass of evidence adduced by Thernstrom and Thernstrom their case rests on a blind-spot. That is their failure to give due recognition to the impact of population movement within the US. Before the Second World War almost 80 per cent of African-Americans lived in the Southern States of the US and most lived in rural contexts. Within 20 years this pattern was to change dramatically as African-Americans moved North and, increasingly, off the land and into the cities. The experience of African-Americans in the Northern cities was quite differ-ent from the situation in the South. In the North segregation was based on residency with African-Americans largely concentrated in specific parts of inner-city areas. This residential segregation allowed for the development of a limited, but nevertheless existent, Black middle-class. Within limits, therefore, there were opportunities in the North for economic upward mobility in a way that did not exist in the South. As more African-Americans moved North, so too the overall economic profile of African-Americans changed. However, this occurred, not because restrictions were being lowered, but rather because an increasing proportion of African-Americans moved to places where more opportunities were available. The educational aspect of this issue was to move in a slightly different direction at this period due to renewed work by the Supreme Court. We will examine this further in the next chapter.

6
From Civil Rights to Afrocentrism and Beyond

Introduction

The previous chapter ended by pointing to the conclusions drawn by the Kerner Commission on the disadvantaged state of African-American communities and their schools in the Northern cities of the US, and the prescription for future action that the Commission recommended. This chapter carries the story forward by examining the way policy and practice developed in two main areas. One of the key education recommendations of the Kerner Commission was that segregation in schools should be reduced, so this will be our first topic to examine. We will begin by looking at the impact of policy in this area and the controversy, particularly due to busing, it engendered. The second issue on which we will concentrate lies in efforts to promote equity between the racial communities, with specific reference to equal opportunity in employment. Quite apart from the importance of this issue in its own right, it is examined here because educational achievement is closely linked to labour market opportunity, and many of the debates over methods of achieving equality centred round educational practices. Thus, for example, many of the key Supreme Court decisions regarding affirmative action dealt with access to educational or training opportunities. Towards the end of the chapter we will flag some of the issues that are of contemporary importance.

As we have seen in the previous chapter, efforts to reduce segregation began in the Southern states of the US. Many of these states had laws and ordinances requiring the provision of separate facilities for African-Americans and Whites, but all of these were cast as illegal as a consequence of the Brown 1954 Supreme Court decision. Despite the conflicts that developed in the celebrated cases of resistance to desegregation, as

in Little Rock, Arkansas, and the University of Mississippi, once segregationist laws were struck down and Southern politicians realised that pressure for desegregation was going to continue from the Federal
authorities, desegregation did proceed apace. Thus, while in 1963/4 only
one per cent of African-American pupils in the Southern states were
attending predominantly White schools, the proportion of African-
American pupils in these schools had risen to 46 per cent by 1972/3.
Orfield and Yun (1999) argue that the peak level of desegregation in the
South was achieved in the late 1980s, but then started to decline as a
consequence of Supreme Court decisions which we will examine further
below.

Tackling segregation in the North

Progress was not so easy, however, in Northern states. In contrast to
the figures for African-American pupils in traditionally White Southern
schools cited above, the comparative proportion of African-American
pupils in schools in Northern states in 1972/3 was 28 per cent. An
important part of the explanation for this difference lay in the different demography of the African-Americans in the Northern and
Southern parts of the country (Garrow, 1993). In the South, African-
Americans and Whites intermingled to a relatively high degree, albeit
that in the segregationist period they had used separate facilities for
many of the day-to-day services of life. Whites owned most of these
services and there was little basis for an African-American middle-class.
Indeed, the Churches provided one of the few social contexts within
which Southern African-Americans maintained some degree of autonomy, which explains why so many of the leaders of the Civil Rights
movement were Ministers. The situation in the North was quite different. Despite the absence of segregationist laws, African-Americans in
Northern cities had become concentrated in particular areas, largely as
a consequence of discrimination in housing: the example of Levittown
was considered in the previous chapter. Within the developing ghettos
of the Northern cities, African-Americans maintained their lives largely
separate and removed from the White populations of the cities. As in
the South they lived separate lives, but, unlike the South, they were
also at a distance with a relatively low level of intermingling of the
communities in everyday life (Spear, 1967; Lemann, 1991).

A combination of residential segregation on the basis of race in the
Northern cities and the tradition of neighbourhood schools resulted in
a high level of educational segregation. While this did not normally

result from specific segregationist laws, there were occasions when actions by schools and other authorities had helped to encourage the development of separate schools for African-American and White communities (Jacobs, 1998). In the South it seemed that segregation was more easily reversed as it was based on laws and ordinances which could be rescinded and communities were much more intermingled. In the Brown case, for example, part of the argument by the plaintiffs had been that the Brown child had to pass an all-White school to attend her all-Black school. Neighbourhood schooling in many parts of the South, in other words, contained an in-built momentum for integration. In the Northern cities, by contrast, something extra was clearly going to be needed, as high levels of residential segregation meant that the continuation of a policy of neighbourhood schools in contained an in-built momentum towards segregated schools. The extra measure that was adopted was to bus pupils across districts in order to mitigate the consequence of residential segregation and create integrated schools. Essentially two approaches were taken to the busing of pupils. The first involved the combination or pairing of two or more schools with different racial compositions in different parts of a school district and the busing of pupils between them. The second type involved the assignment of pupils from an area with one type of racial composition to a school with a different racial composition. In both cases Court-ordered busing for the purpose of desegregation was deemed to be mandatory as it removed school choice from pupils and parents.

Busing

Predictably the introduction of mandatory busing as a means of promoting integration in schools proved to be highly controversial. Equally predictably, it was not long before a series of cases came before the Supreme Court in attempts to clarify the legal basis for busing. This was especially important as attempts to restrict busing through Congress failed to garner sufficient support (Raffel, 1998: pp. 41–45). A series of key Supreme Court decisions set guidelines on who was responsible for busing policy, the conditions in which it could be used and the way it would be implemented. Green vs. County School Board 1969, dealt with a situation where the school authorities argued that priority should be given to parental choice of school. If parents wanted to send their children to particular schools, it was argued, it was not the School Board's responsibility if this resulted in a pattern of segregation. The School Board argued that priority should be given to parental choice despite the fact that, in this instance, a pattern of segregation that had once been enforced by legislation was now maintained almost without change, despite the absence of any enforcing procedures. The Court ruled against the Board and disallowed giving priority to parental choice. The ruling emphasised that the achievement of integration, following the Brown decision, was the clear responsibility of the school authorities. Not only could the Board not seek to avoid that responsibility, but also it should be required to produce a realistic and achievable plan for integration.

Due to the insistence on the need for realistic and achievable plans, the Green ruling was to be of enduring significance for the busing debate, but perhaps the crucial case came with Swann vs. Charlotte-Mecklenburg Board of Education 1971. Whereas the Green decision had concerned a small rural school district, the Swann decision dealt with one of the larger districts in the US involving 84,000 pupils in over 100 schools (Raffel, 1998: pp. 247–249). In this case the Court examined four aspects of busing:

1. was it permissible to use racial balance or quotas for the assignment of pupils?
2. should school authorities pursue the elimination of all-White or all-Black schools?
3. how far should or could school authorities go in rearranging school attendance zones for pupils?
4. what were the limits in the use of transportation policy in pursuit of a remedy to segregation?

The Court ruled that, as transportation had always played a role in educational policy, its use towards the social goal of integration was fully justified. Similarly, despite the relative novelty of using racial statistics in educational policy, the Court felt that this was nevertheless justified in order to establish appropriate targets for action towards integration in a case involving a long-time failure to desegregate. The Court further ruled that the pairing of non-contiguous schools as part of a desegregation policy was permissible even though this need not imply that all single-race schools had to be eliminated from the system:

> All things being equal, with no history of discrimination, it might well be desirable to assign pupils to schools nearest their homes. But all things are not equal in a system that has been deliberately constructed and maintained to enforce racial segregation. ...

Furthermore, the Court ruled that the burden of proof rested with the school authorities to demonstrate that the existence of all-White or all-Black schools was not the result of discrimination. A school system within which illegal segregation was deemed to be occurring was termed a 'dual system' and the purpose of a desegregation plan was to create a 'unitary system'. Following Green, the Swann decision clarified the elements of an acceptable desegregation plan that would allow a school district to be declared unitary. These elements included evidence of the elimination of racial distinctions in student assignment plans, the arrangements for faculty and staff in schools, facilities available in schools, extracurricular activity and transportation.

Thus far we can see, then, that the Supreme Court had established that school authorities were responsible for pursuing the goal of integration, and that it was legal for them to use school transportation as the means and racial statistics to set targets in order to achieve integration. In the Southern states, however, identifying the problem was more straightforward than in the North. As part of the negotiations involved in the passage of the 1964 Civil Rights Act, a difference had been established between *de jure* and *de facto* segregation. *De jure* segregation followed the action of government or state authorities and was, on this basis, deemed to be illegal. *De facto* segregation, on the other hand, was deemed to have occurred by chance or opportunity and was not, therefore, illegal. In the Southern states it was fairly easy to demonstrate that the actually existing segregation in schools was *de jure* rather than *de facto* because most of these states had laws or ordinances requiring or permitting such segregation. In the Northern states, however there was no tradition of 'Jim Crow' laws requiring segregation. This meant that the situation facing the Courts in the Northern states was somewhat more complicated as it was harder to demonstrate intent behind a pattern of segregation.

This was illustrated by one of the first major decisions regarding a school district in the North, Keyes vs. School District No.1, Denver 1973. In this case the District Court agreed that the School Board's action in one part of the district had been illegal in that it had resulted in a pattern of segregated facilities. However, the District Court disagreed that the Board should be required to pursue a desegregation plan across the whole district unless it could be demonstrated that there had been illegal action across the whole district. In other words, the District court was assuming that any segregation in other parts of the district was *de facto* rather than *de jure* until such time as evidence of the latter was provided. However, when the case came to the

Supreme Court the majority overturned this decision on the basis that illegal action by the School Board in one area would necessarily have an impact on other parts of the district. Therefore, the Court ruled, once segregationist intent had been proved in one area, the burden of proof shifted to the School Board to demonstrate that this intent had not occurred elsewhere. This case was important in a number of respects: in particular, it extended the scope of mandatory desegregation to Northern states, affirmed the notion that *de facto* segregation was not illegal and clarified the conditions necessary for creating a court assumption that *de jure* segregation operated.

The tide turns

The liberal tide began to turn, however, with the Milliken vs. Bradley 1974, ruling. This case dealt with a situation that was becoming increasingly typical as Whites moved from the urban areas of cities to the suburbs (Jacobs, 1998). In Detroit this had produced a situation where the metropolitan area of the city was largely comprised of an African-American population, as were the schools, whereas the suburban districts were largely White, again, as were the schools. Furthermore, the boundaries of school districts were co-terminous with this residential pattern, with separate districts covering the metropolitan and suburban areas. This meant that the school authorities for the metropolitan area had no jurisdiction over schools in the suburbs. The issue before the Court revolved around the question of whether cross-district busing could be required in order to achieve integration. The Court divided on the issue. The majority on the Court ruled that cross-district busing could only be used in districts where there was evidence of an actionable problem. In other words, it was not possible to oblige reluctant school authorities to participate in a busing programme unless intent to discriminate on their part could be demonstrated. The minority on the Court argued that the pursuit of integration within the metropolitan area of Detroit was not possible as the districts and schools in the city were predominantly African-American. In other words, restricting the busing policy to the city doomed it to failure as, effectively, there was no-one with whom to integrate. In a later decision in Milliken vs. Bradley 1977, (usually known as Milliken II), the Court permitted the use of state-funded ancillary educational programmes as a component of a desegregation plan where actual pupil desegregation had been blocked. Critics of this decision viewed it as the virtual restoration of the Plessy 'separate but equal' criterion as it could permit school authorities to use additional resources and programmes as a trade-off for desegregation measures (Raffel, 1998: p. 166).

Broadly speaking it is possible to identity two main explanations why this pattern of events had developed. One view, perhaps stated most clearly by Thernstrom and Thernstrom (1997), is that the entire busing strategy proved to be a misguided attempt at demographic engineering that served only to alienate White parents, drive them from metropolitan districts and contribute to a resegregation of schools, particularly in the North. An alternative view is offered by Lomotey and Teddlie (1996) and Orfield and Eaton (1996). They argue that the Courts' shift away from busing was more a consequence of political appointments than a considered assessment of the impact of the strategy. Thus, they argue, the Court that made the original Brown 1954, decision had been appointed by Roosevelt, Truman and Eisenhower, the Court that had handed down the legal basis for busing and other reforming measures reflected the appointments of Kennedy and Johnson, but the 5–4 majority in the Milliken 1974, decision comprised four Justices who had been appointed by President Richard Nixon. Thereafter, all appointments to the Court were made by Republican Presidents Nixon, Reagan or Bush, and it was only well into the term of President Clinton that more liberal appointees were joining the Court (se also McKeever, 1997; Barnum, 1993). If nothing else this highlights the importance of political context on public policy, even in a place such as the US where the final arbiter of policy is said to be based on constitutional imperatives.

The impact of politics on the Court became even more evident through the 1990s as a series of decisions weakened even further the remaining basis for mandatory desegregation plans. In Board of Education of Oklahoma City vs. Dowell 1991, the Court ruled that the school board had to act 'to the best extent possible' to meet the Green criteria, but that the authority of District Court oversight could not be indefinite. In Freeman vs. Pitts 1992, the Court accepted that compliance with the Green criteria could proceed in stages and that District Court authority could be removed bit by bit. This decision went further to accept evidence of good faith on the part of school boards and to accept that there were practical limits to what could be achieved. In other words, when the conditions under which the original court order had been issued were addressed, then the school board had no continuing requirement to tackle segregation arising from any subsequent demographic changes. In Missouri vs. Jenkins 1995, the

Supreme Court overturned a District Court decision on the conditions that were required for a school board to demonstrate the success of a segregation plan. The District Court had argued that the success of the desegregation plan had to be demonstrated by successful outcomes for minority pupils and that outcomes were best judged by academic achievement. By contrast, the Supreme Court took the view that, since many other factors influenced student achievement, a pattern of difference on this alone was insufficient to demonstrate continuing *de jure*, and hence illegal, segregation. The Supreme Court went further to argue that a swift return to local control was desirable, thereby making it easier for School Boards to gain a declaration of unitary status and escape from District Court oversight of mandatory desegregation plans. All of these decisions came from a period when the balance of the Court had shifted even more firmly to the right during the Republican Presidencies of Reagan and Bush.

Alternative routes to integration

While busing was the predominant strategy towards integration, it was not the only approach. An alternative strategy, the original rationale for which got somewhat lost in later years when market principles became more important in education (Cohn, 1997), was based on the encouragement of parental choice. 'Magnet' schools were designed as specialist institutions, usually with extra resources, which aimed to encourage the return of White pupils to inner-city schools (Dougherty and Sostre, 1992). The film 'Fame' is perhaps the best-known example of a magnet school, and it exemplifies the type in that the strategy aimed to produce schools that were attractive enough to enable voluntary integration by choice. Ascher (1993) suggested that by the 1990s this 'voluntary' strategy had become the predominant approach to the promotion of desegregation, even though the evidence for its efficacy was mixed. Thus, for example, research reported by Wells (2002) and Metz (1986) questioned whether many or most parents chose schools on the basis of educational quality, while Fife (1992) suggested that the level of segregation was more likely to be reduced in circumstances where desegregation was mandatory rather than voluntaristic. More recently choice advocates argued that if parents, particularly those from disadvantaged backgrounds, were to be given school vouchers then they could gain access to better schools, and that this might break down some of the inequities created by residential segregation. This case was given a boost by the Supreme Court decision in Zelman vs. Simmons-Harris 2002, in which a voucher scheme in Cleveland was deemed to be legal even though parents could use the vouchers to gain access to private denominational schools. Although the implications of this ruling are not yet clear (Kemerer, 2002; Pallas, 2002), the available evidence suggests the main consequence is to subsidise parents who already use private denominational schools, rather than to draw in large numbers of new parents who are fleeing from public schools (Wells, 2002). If accurate, this would place a question-mark over the claim that this form of choice encourages desegregation.

The positive effects derived from busing centred on the claim to have broken the cycle of segregation where this had created a situation where all-Black institutions could be labelled as inferior and less adequate than their White equivalents – clearly desegregation would remove this attribution. But there was some evidence also that desegregation helped to raise the expectations of African-American students, and arguably, it provided some, at least, with the opportunity to break into networks that would otherwise have been foreclosed to them. However, the case for busing was further weakened by Jencks' (1972) argument that the gains on student achievement as a consequence of desegregation were not, in fact, that significant:

> While desegregation will almost certainly reduce the overall level of variation in test scores, the reduction will probably be quite small. Most cognitive inequality is within racial groups, within economic groups, and within schools. Desegregation will not affect these disparities much. (Jencks, 1972: p. 106).

The general argument, arising from Jencks' work and other studies at the time, was that schools did not have as big an impact on pupil performance in comparison with other social factors. This view has since been altered in the light of new evidence and analysis, but at the time it suggested that the time and energy devoted to desegregation might be of intrinsic, social value, but was of little educational value. However, the biggest negative on the story to date lies in the contemporary pattern where, despite all the efforts that have taken place over the years, the level of segregation in American schools remains stubbornly high and is, if anything, increasing (McQuillan and Donato, 1999; Reardon, et al., 1999), with little evidence of any active countervailing measures designed to reverse this pattern (Orfield and Yun, 1999).

Discrimination and affirmative action

The second main area we wish to explore in this chapter concerns the provision of equality. In the previous chapter we have already seen the importance of equality in US policy because of the centrality of this concept in the US Constitution and, more particularly, the 14th Amendment. However, debates on the meaning of the concept and its realisation in practice, have continued over time, up to and beyond the Kerner Commission. A key area of debate, in the US and elsewhere, lies in the field of employment opportunity. Education has played a fundamental part in this discussion because of the link between access to educational opportunity, academic achievement and labour market opportunity. Even more particularly in the US case, special measures to achieve greater employment equality, through affirmative action, have directly involved access to educational institutions. We will examine the development of these issues below, but first we will look briefly at the employment process in order to highlight certain aspects of potential discrimination.

When we think of discrimination in employment we often tend to focus on decisions made at the point of selection. That we do this is unsurprising since this is the point at which the applicants for a job are differentiated between those to whom an opportunity will be offered and those to whom it will not. But the point of selection is only the end-point of a series of stages and the cause of unfair or arbitrary discrimination may be located at any one of those stages. A simple representation of the stages involved in employment decisions might begin with a population who will provide the basis for a theoretical pool of applicants for a job opportunity. Usually the potential pool of applicants will be defined by criteria of qualifications or experience. Given that this is so, the social distribution of qualifications or experience becomes an important factor. If the level of qualifications is differentially distributed across a number of social groups, this may have the effect of making it easier for some people than others to avail of the job opportunity. Similarly, if there is a high level of segregation in the labour market, with some social groups being over-represented in particular sectors of employment, then the level of experience which members of social groups can call upon may also differ. In other words, when qualifications or work experience are not evenly distributed across social groups in a population, then setting them as criteria for a job opportunity will mean that members of those social groups may have differential access to the opportunity.

A second stage arises from the fact that not everyone who is in the potential pool of applicants for a job opportunity will actually apply for that job opportunity. Unfair or arbitrary discrimination can occur in at least two separate conditions. First, if knowledge about the job opportunity is not equally available to potential applicants, then members of some social groups may be denied the ability to apply for that opportunity. This could occur in a situation where members of a particular social group were over-represented within a workplace and opportunities for new recruits were advertised through informal networks, such as word-of-mouth contacts. Second, even when the opportunity is widely and formally advertised, if members of a social group believe that they are likely to be discriminated against, or that they will be poorly treated by other employees, they may decide it is not worth their while applying for the opportunity. Both conditions will result in a difference between the social profile of actual applicants and the potential pool of applicants.

The third stage arises when we move from the point of application to short-listing for interview. Experience suggests that more formal and empirical short-listing procedures are less likely to result in unfair or arbitrary discrimination against particular groups of people (McCrudden, 1992). As we shall see below, there have been debates in the US on the extent to which employers could use test results to differentiate between applicants for jobs or other opportunities. The danger of unfair discrimination rises in proportion to the extent to which subjective criteria are permitted to play a role. The final stage of the recruitment process is the point of selection, when the short-listed candidates are (usually) interviewed and selected. Once again, unfair or arbitrary discrimination is less likely to occur when the procedures are formalised and empirical.

The main point of this short discussion of employment processes is simply to highlight the fact that a differential pattern of outcomes between members of different social groups at the selection stage may be a consequence of factors operating at a number of different points. If an employer finds, for example, that more Protestants than Catholics are being recruited, this may be because of action at the point of selection, at the short-listing stage, at the advertising stage or because of the criteria which were set for the job opportunity in the first place. The diagnosis of a problem would need to be aware of the range of possible problems. Overarching it all, however, is the basic definition of discrimination as the situation where one person is treated less favourably than another on grounds that are arbitrary and irrelevant to the opportunity for which those people were being considered. Direct discrimination occurs when there is intent to treat one person less favourably than another on arbitrary grounds. However, discrimination may also be indirect if a criterion is set for applicants which has the effect of making it much easier for one type of person to avail of the opportunity than another, and which is not relevant to the opportunity under consideration. Indirect discrimination may occur whether or not intent to discriminate exists. Of course, it is important to highlight also that different states may adopt different legal definitions of what constitutes illegal discrimination. In those states where anti-discrimination laws operate, they will always include direct discrimination, but may or may not cover indirect discrimination. Also, discrimination can occur on the grounds of gender, religion, racial, ethnic or linguistic origin, marital status or sexual orientation: discrimination on the basis of any or all of these may be deemed illegal.

In the US the basis for defining illegal discrimination is linked directly to judicial interpretation of the meaning and scope of the Constitution. In addition to the basic issues discussed above, it is possible also to discern an evolving pattern in US policy where the practical definition of equality has shifted from a notion of equality of opportunity, through equality of participation, to equality of outcome. Equality of opportunity implies that action be taken to remove arbitrary or unfair barriers to participation. To focus on equality of participation, on the other hand, implies that a measured level of statistical parity in participation be achieved. This may only be achieved by going beyond the removal of barriers to the active encouragement of participation by targeted groups. The strongest version of equality is based on the idea of equality of outcome. This condition implies a measured level of statistical parity in the final outcomes and requires the highest level of intervention.

A Supreme Court ruling illustrates one of the ways in which this issue was addressed. In Lau vs. Nicols 1974, the Court was asked to rule on the treatment provided to children of Chinese origin in San Francisco (Howe, 1989; Tollet, 1982). The plaintiffs wanted to receive their education in Chinese. The school authorities argued that 'equal treatment' in this case implied that the children were treated exactly the same as any other children under their jurisdiction. In other words, if all children were educated through English, then it was appropriate to educate the Chinese children through English as well. Contrary to this argument, the Court ruled that equal treatment did not imply absolute equivalence in treatment:

> Under these state-imposed standards there is no equal treatment merely by providing...the same facilities, textbooks, teachers and curriculum; for students who do not understand English are effectively foreclosed from any meaningful education.

In making this ruling the Court rejected a formal definition of equality, but rather linked the provision of equality to the outcomes of that provision. In this particular instance, the Court accepted that it was an occasion where it was necessary to treat some people differently in order to achieve equality (Burbules, 1990; Howe, 1990).

This example highlights an aspect of the practical issues involved in the achievement of equality. In a somewhat broader sense, this issue has been explored and debated in the issue of affirmative action, that is, the use of special measures in order to achieve equality. One of the reasons the concept of affirmative action excites such controversy is precisely because it can mean many different things to different people, quite apart from the differing legal bases for affirmative action in different jurisdictions. McCrudden (1986) has outlined a typology of measures which help to delineate the various ways in which affirmative action has been put into practice in different places and at different times.

First, it is necessary that discrimination be deemed to be illegal on some basis or other as discussed above. Legislation of this kind will cover direct discrimination, but may also determine that indirect discrimination is illegal. Usually the proscription of discrimination is accompanied by the establishment of some body that is responsible for encouraging compliance with the law, and there may be a separate body with the responsibility of dealing with allegations of discrimination. Second, the simplest form of affirmative action, beyond the legal proscription of discrimination, is for outreach measures. These are measures that are designed to encourage greater participation by previously under-represented groups. They might include special information programmes or even special training programmes. In the present context the most important aspect of outreach measures is that they operate up to, but not at, the point of selection. The main rational of this approach is to try and create an equal playing field at the point of selection.

A third point along the scale lies with the use of criteria which are *de jure* neutral, in that they are not directly based on group membership, but which, *de facto*, are over-inclusive of previously under-represented groups. For example, if African-Americans are under-represented in a workplace and are over-represented among the unemployed, then using unemployment as a criterion would over-include African-Americans as eligible for an opportunity even though it would not exclude non-African-Americans. The fourth point on the scale is explicitly to give preferential treatment to members of a previously under-represented group in order to reduce that under-representation. The simplest form of preferential treatment is to use some mechanism like the 'tie-break' so that, all other things being equal between two candidates, the opportunity would be offered to the one from the under-represented group. Another variant on this is to use the 'minimax' principle whereby minimum requirements are set for an opportunity, qualifications above the minimum do not confer any additional advantage and race or other factors can come into play for all those who meet the minimum conditions. A stronger version of this approach would be to determine quotas for defined social groups so that regardless of the absolute ranking between candidates, a set proportion of places would be held for members of an under-represented group.

The use of over-inclusive or preferential criteria highlights the controversial nature of affirmative action, as they appear to run counter to the merit principle. This is usually defined as the idea that any particular opportunity should be offered first to the most meritorious candidate, and that any ranking of candidates should be based on strictly job-related criteria. To use neutral, but over-inclusive criteria, or to give preferential treatment, is to use criteria that lie outwith this. The fifth, and final, point on McCrudden's scale is to redefine the concept of merit in order to include within its remit criteria that would have the effect on increasing the participation and/or success of candidates from particular backgrounds. McCrudden (1996) extended this discussion by highlighting the variety of meaning that, in practice, exists within the notion of merit itself.

This discussion highlights some of the key themes that have informed debates on the concept of equality, how it should be understood and defined and, perhaps most importantly, how it should be put into practice. In the US we have already seen how the Supreme Court placed a central role in defining the limits and possibilities of government action in the process of desegregating schools. This was also in the Court's role in establishing the legal limits and possibilities for measures that were designed to achieve equality. Thus, for example, in the case of Griggs vs. The Duke Power Company 1971, the Court considered the use of selection tests which were shown to have an adverse impact on minority racial groups. The question before the Court was whether or not the company could use these tests as part of the selection process. In this case the Court ruled that the use of tests with a demonstrable adverse impact on minorities should be deemed to be discriminatory, unless and until the employer using the test for selection purposes was able to demonstrate its validity for the specific job, to the satisfaction of the Court. This strong stance by the Court was mitigated a little by a later ruling in Washington vs. Davis 1976, in which the use of a racially neutral criterion which had a demonstrable differential racial impact, could not in itself be taken as evidence of discrimination unless there was some evidence of intent to discriminate. In this case the responsibility for demonstrating intent lay with the plaintiff.

Both cases illustrate the role played by the Supreme Court in defining policy, and show how this evolved and changed over time. In the area of affirmative action and, more specifically, the controversial issue of quotas, three cases in the latter part of the 1970s played a key role in setting the basis for policy and practice until very recently. Each of the cases dealing with entry to college or a training opportunity, tested the limits of affirmative action designed to promote the interests of previously under-represented minorities and highlighted the position of excluded members of the majority group. The first case, DeFunis vs. the University of Washington 1977, involved a White applicant to the university who was turned down. Other applicants with lower grades than DeFunis gained entry to the college through a special access programme that retained a proportion of places for minorities. DeFunis argued that his right to equal treatment was being abrogated by this affirmative action measure, while the university argued that the special access programme enhanced the collective utility to the university and society. The Court ordered that DeFunis should be permitted onto the course while the case was being considered. However, before judgement could be offered he completed the course and the judgement was declared moot. It was only a matter of time, however, before a similar case would come up for consideration.

This second key case concerned the Regents of the University of California vs. Bakke 1978. The university operated a 16 per cent quota for entry to its medical school. Bakke had been denied entry to the course even though he had achieved higher grades in comparison with some of those who entered through the minority quota. As it was relevant to the case it should be noted that the successful applicants through the quota scheme had all achieved defined minimum levels of performance. In a complex judgement, in which six different views were offered, the Court was divided amongst those who agreed with the legality of using race as a factor in entry decisions and those who did not. The swing vote was to allow for the use of race, but only under strict conditions. In particular, there had to be clear evidence of past discrimination, a compelling interest in using race for ameliorative purposes and the use of race should be narrowly tailored to meet this need. Due to the variety of views among the Justices, the legal position of racially-based affirmative action became very unclear, to the extent that a virtual moratorium was declared on their use. The situation was clarified a little after the decision in the third case, United Steel Workers of America vs. Weber 1979. This case dealt with a special training programme on which half of all the places were reserved for minorities. As with the previous cases, this one was brought by a White who had failed to get onto the programme and who sought to have the use of reserved places deemed illegal. In this case the Court ruled that affirmative action measures that involved the use of numerical goals and targets, but not rigid quotas, were permissible. This decision allowed the restoration of special admission programmes. These programmes now had to use goals and targets for minority participation, but could not use rigid quotas for minorities to be filled regardless of any other factors. In attempting to meet goals and targets it was deemed to be legal to set lower admission standards as long as minimum standards were also set and met. These cases lead to the establishment of 'strict scrutiny' criteria for special admissions programmes, which implied the need for a compelling interest for a narrowly tailored programme.

Although President Nixon had opposed busing and appointed conservative Supreme Court Justices who set about dismantling the framework established by their more liberal predecessors, Nixon did implement a preference programme towards the start of his first term. This measure was designed to promote the development of an entrepreneurial class among the African-American community by requiring a proportion of activity arising from federal programmes to be 'set-aside' for minorities (Jacoby, 1998: p. 381). The legality of these set-aside programmes was confirmed by the Supreme Court in Fullilove vs. Klutznick 1980, in which the Court rejected a claim by contractors against a requirement that ten per cent of the work on federal contracts should go to minority owned firms.

The period during which these cases were held helped to highlight the controversial nature of affirmative action measures and allows us to summarise the basic case for and against these special measures. Those who opposed these measures argued that discrimination on any basis was always wrong and, therefore, that all policy should be 'blind' to group membership criteria. Affirmative action, by its very nature, gives some account to these dimensions. A second argument against affirmative action is that the remedies have an unfair impact. In particular, the negative effect of these measures is felt by present generations, even though any fault that they seek to redress is the responsibility of previous generations. A third criticism is that affirmative action measures, probably as a consequence of the previous two objections, only serve to exacerbate intergroup tensions. The fourth, and final, criticism to be mentioned here is the claim that the practical experience of affirmative action is that it contains an in-built momentum towards stronger and more extreme measures over time, as each level of action is seen not to work (Glazar, 1975; Bullivant, 1992).

The arguments in favour of affirmative action remain largely as they were. That is, it provides a basis for redressing and providing compensation for past wrongs (Little and Robbins, 1982) and it provides for a diverse environment within which better understanding and reduced prejudice will be possible. In so doing it recognises that a simple declaration that discrimination is illegal merely places everyone in an equal competition from that point on, but does not necessarily mean that everyone starts the competition from the same position. A second argument in favour of affirmative action is that by enhancing the participation and success of previously under-represented groups we are contributing to the enhancement of distributive justice. This will contribute to the perception and actuality of a fair society, which will in turn contribute to the collective interest by rendering society more stable. A third and final argument in favour of affirmative action lies in the collective benefit to be gained by utilising the skills and abilities of all members of society. One of the biggest drawbacks of discrimination, apart from its injustice, lies in the way it leads a society to underuse its own people. Affirmative action, by redressing the effects of past discrimination, and creating a new context where everyone feels valued and involved, provides the best chance to use effectively the collective resource of society.

During the years of the Reagan and Bush administrations, official support for affirmative action and related measures waned considerably. As more conservative appointees were placed on the Supreme Court, it was no surprise that, over time, a number of Court judgements weakened the scope of affirmative action. This occurred both by setting tougher criteria before an affirmative action programme could be put in place and also by making it easier to avoid the need for special measures. Despite this, the use of affirmative action had by then become almost routine for most large employers in the US. Edwards (1995) has described the eight stages to an affirmative action plan. These include an analysis of current workforces in terms of the participation levels of ethnic, racial and gender groups; an analysis of the number of qualified and available minorities that could, in theory, be employed in the workplace; a utilisation analysis which compares the availability pattern with the workforce pattern, and identifies a problem if current participation for a group is less than 80 per cent of its possible participation; the establishment and annual review of goals and timetables in order to redress any identified under-utilisation; and finally, the identification of specific measures to achieve the goals.

Further evidence of the apparent ubiquity of affirmative action seemed to follow the Supreme Court decision in Wards Cove Packing Company vs. Antonio 1989, which restricted the use of statistical comparisons, as Congress almost immediately reversed this decision in the 1991 Civil Rights Act. Nevertheless the 1990s saw a renewed assault on affirmative action on a number of fronts (Jacoby, 1998). In Richmond vs. JA Croson 1989, some restrictions were placed on the use of set-aside programmes by states and local governments and this constraint was extended to federal programmes by the decision in Adarand vs. Pena 1995. Although these decisions did not outlaw set-aside measures, it required the application of the tighter 'strict scrutiny' conditions that had been established for university admissions programmes. President Clinton's response was to reaffirm the commitment of his administration to affirmative action (Clinton, 1995), but on the basis of a 'mend it, don't end it' approach. While he highlighted the extent to which the problems linked to the consequences of discrimination have been dealt with, notwithstanding the continuing need to tackle these problems, he set out four criteria which were to inform his administration's approach to affirmative action:

> No quotas in theory or practice; no illegal discrimination of any kind, including reverse discrimination; no preference for people who are not qualified for any job or other opportunity; and as soon as a program has succeeded, it must be retired. Any program that doesn't meet these four principles must be eliminated or reformed to meet them. (Clinton, 1995).

He ended by contrasting the longevity of the problem with the recent origins of ameliorative measures:

> The job of ending discrimination in this country is not over. That should not be surprising. We had slavery for centuries before the passage of the 13th, 14th and 15th Amendments. We waited another hundred years for the civil rights legislation. Women have had the vote for less than a hundred years. ... If properly done, affirmative action can help us come together, go forward and grow together. It is in our moral, legal and practical interest to see that every person can make the most of his life. In the fight for the future, we need all hands on deck and some of those hands still need a helping hand. (Clinton, 1995).

However, this speech was perhaps the only significant intervention made by President Clinton on the issue of affirmative action. He did attempt to encourage a wider discussion by running a year long initiative on race issues, but this had limited impact. Furthermore, the conservative backlash against affirmative action was not yet over. In Podberesky vs. Kirwan 1994, a lower court had decided that a special scholarship programme at the University of Maryland for African-American students was unconstitutional. The Supreme Court declined to hear arguments in this case thereby letting the Podberesky ruling stand. Perhaps even more significant, in Hopwood vs. Texas 1996, a different lower court basically overturned the Bakke ruling when it decided that the University of Texas Law School had fulfilled its obligation to redress the effects of racial discrimination and that therefore there was no compelling reason to maintain race as a factor in admissions decisions. Once again the Supreme Court declined to hear argument on the case thereby letting the ruling stand (for alternative views on this see Thernstrom and Thernstrom, 1997; and Orfield and Miller, 1998). In 1995 the Regents of the University of California voted to end the use of racial preferences in admissions decisions and in the following years, in a referendum on Proposition 209, California voters ended the use of race as a factor in affirmative action programmes. One of the more significant aspects of these decisions is that they have occurred in the states with the largest and growing concentration of Latino minorities. While the decisions have prompted explorations of alternative methods of redressing the effects of discrimination, there is no doubt that already their impact can be seen in a dramatic fall in the number of minority admissions to higher education (Orfield and Miller, 1998).

The support of the Clinton administration for affirmative action, however limited, and its *de facto* acceptance as routine by most businesses in the US, had both suggested that the debates on anti-discrimination measures were settled. Clearly this was incorrect as debates on affirmative action have been re-ignited, perhaps not least by the increasing size of the minority populations in the US and, more particularly, the increase in the Latino community. Furthermore, the result of the 2001 presidential race was seen as crucial by many as the winner was likely to have an opportunity to make some appointments to the Supreme Court and thereby influence the tenor of social policy for many years to come. That George W. Bush emerged as the President led many to expect a restoration or confirmation of the conservative position on the Court. However, as Eisenhower had found in a previous age, it is not always possible to predict the outcomes of the Justices' deliberations simply on the basis of assumed political positions.

This was dramatically demonstrated in a Supreme Court decision in 2003 concerning two White students who were unsuccessful in gaining entry to the University of Michigan undergraduate programme and to the university's Law School respectively. Prior to the Bakke decision it was clear that affirmative action was justified when there was evidence of discrimination in previous admissions systems. The main issue tested at the Bakke case was whether the maintenance of diversity was itself a compelling interest above and beyond any remediation goals. Although the Bakke decision was, as we saw above, somewhat unclear, the main conclusion to emerge from it was that diversity did represent a compelling interest, but that any affirmative action had to be tailored to meet this end. It was on this basis that the idea of quotas had been disallowed. The Hopwood decision seemed to remove the compelling interest accorded to diversity and left remediation as the sole justification for affirmative action, but this case had not been taken by the Supreme Court. The two Michigan cases did allow for this issue to be addressed.

The majority on the Court provoked some surprise when it ruled that the goal of diversity was a compelling interest for universities and hence affirmative action could be justified on that basis. However, the Court also ruled that any affirmative action measures had to be narrowly tailored to that goal and that the use of race as a criterion for admissions decisions had to be placed within a holistic assessment of individual applicants, rather than as a procedure which provided specific advantage to applicants solely on the basis of their racial membership. On this basis the Court ruled that the University of Michigan could use race in its admissions procedure, but that the specific mechanism used for undergraduate admissions (which involved a points system in which minority applicants received a set number of points due to their minority status) was not acceptable, while the procedure used by the Law School (which involved a holistic assessment of individual applicants within which race was one of the factors taken into account) was acceptable. The Court encouraged universities to investigate the use of race-neutral admissions systems, but did not require them to pursue these in an exhaustive way. Also, it identified the compelling interest of diversity as a legitimate policy option rather than a legal imperative, thereby permitting policy decisions – such as the California referendum effectively banning affirmative action – which decided one way or the other on the pursuit of this goal. Thus, the Michigan decision seems to have underpinned the legal basis for affirmative action that had been in place since the Bakke decision, while at the same time tightening the conditions under which race can be used within admissions procedures.

The 'school wars'

In parallel with some of the trends noted above, the debate over race and education developed in a third direction with a focus on the curriculum and the debate over 'political correctness'. On one level this debate was carried out within universities and centred round the appropriate canon of literature. For some the canon was the archive of traditional literature that embodied the cultural values of civilisation (Bloom, 1994). For others the canon comprised the works of 'dead white European men' offering a one-sided account of universalism. In a plural society, and an increasingly plural academy, the critics argued, the canon should reflect the wider plurality of voices and experience (Dunant, 1994). The traditionalists felt that the radical critic were offering a debased culture replete with debased language, and painted a picture of the 'politically correct' 'thought police' roaming the universities to prevent crimes against pluralism. One such critic was Hughes (1993), who combined his attack on the left with an equally focused attack on the debasement of language by the political right, in particular the sound-bite simplicities of the Reagan era and the three 'fs' of US right-wing politics: flag, foetus and family.

More relevant for present concerns was the battle over the school curriculum (Schlesinger, 1991; Berube, 1994; Glazar, 1997). Three distinct positions were present in this debate. One side comprised the Afro-centrists who tried to define a new curriculum that placed Africa at the centre of history and offered a radical break with the Eurocentric curriculum of mainstream education. A second group rose to challenge the challengers. They comprised Western Traditionalists who clung to some version of the 'melting pot' to the extent that they still wished to define a common American culture, based on western civilisation, democratic practice and civic symbols, and inculcated to all pupils through the schools. The Traditionalists attacked the Afrocentrists for their alleged use of history as therapy, but in truth spent much of their time setting up and demolishing straw men. The third group, which existed somewhere between the other two, comprised multiculturalists who advocated the value and richness of diversity, accepted the need for a more diverse and plural curriculum, but nevertheless did not want to abandon the democratic ideals of western development. After all, they said, multiculturalism itself has developed within this context. The culture wars, may have provoked an extraordinary amount of coverage in newspapers and magazines, but away from the hype and exaggeration, multiculturalism in the US has actually been about the widening of the curriculum in order to promote a more inclusive society. The irony is that this multiculturalist approach has been established in a context where the level of segregation in schools was widening and the level of participation of minorities in higher education was reducing.

7
'Race' and Education in Britain

Introduction

Although the United Kingdom is a single political unit, it contains four administrative jurisdictions for education in England, Wales, Scotland and Northern Ireland. While the broad patterns of educational development have followed similar paths in all four areas, there are, nevertheless, important differences between them; differences which arguably are widening since the establishment of devolved Assemblies in Scotland and Wales. In Northern Ireland religious divisions in the society have been mirrored by the development of separate school systems for Catholics and Protestants. Separate Catholic schools exist also in Britain, or the other three areas of the UK, but outside Northern Ireland these schools comprise a relatively small component of the education system. Furthermore, the mainstream school system in Britain, by and large, does not reflect a specifically Protestant ethos. In Northern Ireland this is not the case, as we will see in Chapter 9.

At least from the 1960s onwards educationalists in Britain have grappled with the reality of an increasingly polyethnic society and a variety of strategies have been adopted. The initial strategy sought to incorporate, or assimilate, ethnic minorities into an assumed 'British way of life'. When this strategy was abandoned the two main subsequent strategies, multiculturalism and the anti-racism, operated within a broadly inclusive framework in which an attempt was made to accommodate ethnic minorities. However, education reforms in the 1990s emphasised managerial and administrative concerns within a market-led competitive approach to educational provision, and generally saw a reduced level of official interest in interventions for specifically social ends. In this period attention was drawn towards attempts to establish separate schools for particular ethnic communities, most notably the Islamic community. Advocates of separate Islamic schools pointed to the existence of separate Catholic and Jewish schools, never mind schools that offered a specifically denominational character for Protestant groups, and argued that they should be treated no differently. The election of the Labour government in 1997, after sixteen years of Conservative rule, led some to hope for a restoration of broader social goals within education policy, although others were more sanguine in their expectations. In the event, the 'third way' advocated by Tony Blair, incorporated a mix of public and private sector approaches that was leavened by a commitment to social justice rather than centrally driven by such a commitment. This chapter outlines this evolution of policy.

Ethnic pluralism in Britain

It is sometimes assumed that Britain has only recently become a multi-ethnic society. This is far from the case. Thus, for example, Blacks are known to have been in Britain in 1555, that is, before the birth of Shakespeare and before the arrival of the potato. That said, it is the case that post-Second World War inward migration to Britain provided the primary basis for movement towards education policy on pluralism. Significantly this occurred in the period when post-war reconstruction was happening, including the establishment of free and compulsory second level education. Underpinning this reconstruction was a discourse of equal opportunity through social mobility, at least for those of the British nation whose opportunities for social advancement had been constrained. At least initially this discourse of equality did not seem to extend to the newly arrived migrants.

The most significant source of migrants to Britain in the period 1945–54 was from Europe, in particular Ireland, and they faced a relatively liberal attitude at an official level. This contrasted with the fears expressed about the social and racial problems that were seen as linked to the arrival of Black migrants from former colonial territories who were British subjects:

> It was during the period from 1945–62 that the terms of political debate about coloured immigration were established, leading to a close association between race and immigration in both policy debates and in popular and media discourses. (Solomos, 1992: p. 10).

The discourse linking race and immigration defined the 'new' Black Britons as the problem and focused on ways of trying to control or limit their entry to Britain. Solomos (1992) points out that the debates were not just about the supposed characteristics of the Black migrants, but also on their effect on the racial character of the British people and national identity. Additionally, in the 1950s the official Government position appeared to be that no educational interventions were either necessary or possible to deal with racial prejudice and negative stereotypes (Richmond, 1984/6).

In the 1960s this position evolved towards the adoption of an explicitly assimilationist strategy in education. This strategy was based on the belief that Britain was a culturally homogeneous society into which inward migrants ought to be inculcated. The view was clearly expressed in the Second Report of the Commonwealth Immigrant Advisory Council:

> A national system of education must aim at producing citizens who can take their place in society properly equipped to exercise rights and perform duties the same as those of other citizens. If their parents were brought up in another culture and another tradition, children should be encouraged to respect it, but a national system cannot be expected to perpetuate the different values of immigrant groups. (Cited in Mullard, 1985: p. 40).

Discriminatory housing practices had encouraged the concentration of Black migrant families, particularly in inner-city areas. Despite this, the assimilationist underpinnings of policy at the time cast it as undesirable that Black children be concentrated in particular schools. It was felt that their lack of fluency in English might have held back the education of White children. Reflecting this view, the Minister of Education said, in the House of Commons in November 1963, that, 'if possible, it is desirable on education grounds that no one school should have more than about 30 per cent of immigrants'. DES circular 7/65 introduced a policy of dispersal aimed at migrant children to ensure that such concentrations did not occur and provided a clear indication to the minority groups that Local Education Authorities (LEAs) identified them as the problem:

> In fact, however, it was the 'solution' itself which created the real problem. Busing proved to be a great physical burden and resulted in many Black children being deprived of a normal childhood.

Basically, the policy of 'dispersal' put up to three hours on their working day and on the working day of their mothers and fathers ... The distance between home and school meant that parents were unable to take as much interest in their children's schooling as they might have done with a neighbouring school. The disenchantment of many non-whites with British schooling can be traced back to the bitterness engendered by Circular 7/65. (Nixon, 1984/6: 23).

By the early 1970s the dispersal policy was officially abandoned, but, as Nixon suggests, the damage was by then done. Further disenchantment on the part of minority parents was created by the number of West Indian children placed in Educationally Subnormal (ESN) schools (Coard, 1971). More generally, the view came to be held by many Black parents that schools were somehow or other failing Black children thus limiting their life opportunities (Tomlinson, 1985; Bhachu, 1984/6).

As the focus of concerns began to shift, so too did the policy towards the contribution of education. In 1966 Roy Jenkins argued that what was required was 'not a flattening process of assimilation but equal opportunity, accompanied by cultural diversity, in an atmosphere of mutual tolerance' (cited in Mullard, 1985: p. 44). In the 1970s then, official policy moved from an assimilationist strategy to an integrationist strategy, where the latter was less overtly racist in approach and, rhetorically at least, was guided by the notion of 'unity through diversity'. The integrationist approach encouraged schools to accommodate, to some degree, cultural diversity within the curriculum. There were, however, limits to this accommodation, as expressed in a Select Committee Report on Education in 1973:

The demand for black studies has arisen because the content of education in Britain is seen as Anglo centric and biased against Black people. We can understand this. But we doubt whether black studies in the narrow sense would make a contribution to wider education and better race relations and we are not attracted by the idea of black teachers teaching black pupils in separate classes or establishments. ... We come down firmly on the side of unity through diversity.

The multicultural approach developed from this to argue that schools should not only reflect minority cultures, but also should provide a positive self-image for Black pupils and encourage greater tolerance among White pupils. The primary focus of the multicultural approach was on attitudes and prejudice, with the view that the sympathetic teaching of other cultures would dispel the myths and ignorance that provided the basis for prejudice (Rattansi, 1992: pp. 24–25). To some, however, this approach abstracted culture from the wider social context of a racist society:

> ...the focus was on the ethnic and cultural life styles of black pupils rather than the wider political culture in which their life styles were to be determined. The 3Ss interpretation of multicultural education (Saris, Samosas and Steel bands) subordinated political realities to cultural artefacts. (Troyna, 1992: p. 74).

By the 1980s the culturalist emphasis of early versions of multicultural education were hotly debated (see articles in *New Community*, Volume 10 (1982/3), by Fenton, Saunders, Milner, Richards, James, Troyna and Dolan) with many arguing for a more explicitly anti-racist dimension to educational interventions:

> ...a growing body of opinion began to press for 'anti-racist teaching', resulting in the 'cultural' and 'racial' strands of the argument slowly drawing apart. This polarisation has continued as teachers who feared that anti-racist teaching might be more political than educational ... took refuge under the umbrella of multiculturalism. ... Multiculturalism can be retrieved from the confection it has become ... by making the 'cultural' element (past and present) mean what it is supposed to mean: 'ways of life' for black people in this society include ways of living with racism, and ways of resisting it. (Milner, 1982/3: p. 73)

In 1983 the anti-racist theme was taken up by the Inner London Education Authority (ILEA) and , following support from the Commission for Racial Equality, by a number of other Local Education Authorities (LEAs) in Britain (Hiro, 1992: p. 230). In practice, educational initiatives at this stage began to take on a mixture of anti-racist and multiculturalist themes, both of which were reflected in the landmark Swann Report, Education For All, published in 1985.

The Swann Committee had been established by the Labour Government in 1979, originally under the Chair of Lord Rampton. The task given to the Committee was to investigate the attainment of ethnic minority pupils in Britain and to ascertain the reasons for any pattern of underachievement they might find. Given the controversy over the attainment levels of Afro-Caribbean pupils, the Committee decided to focus on this issue first, and then to cover the wider range of minority communities. The interim report, published in 1981, concluded that the underachievement of Afro-Caribbean children was largely due to racism in society and the education system (Parekh, 1992: p. 97). By the time this report was published, however, the Labour government had been replaced by the first Thatcher government and Sir Keith Joseph was the Minister for Education. Although the Conservative government had not yet established a clear policy for education, its inclination was towards the introduction of markets rather than state intervention, and there was no evident enthusiasm for Rampton's report or recommendations. In the event the main consequence was that Lord Rampton was replaced as Chair of the Committee by Lord Swann. The Committee then continued with its task of examining evidence on the attainment patterns of a wide range of ethnic minorities in Britain including children of Chinese, Cypriot, Italian, Ukrainian, Vietnamese and Traveller origins. The final report also included sections on teacher education, multicultural education and language policy.

The Swann Report, published in 1985, retreated somewhat from the position taken in the interim report (Little, 1984/6: p. 228) although it still stressed the role of racism in society:

> ...the fact remains that racism in society at large, and operating through employers, trade unions, landlords, and housing authorities, not to mention racial harassment and violence, contributes to this extra dimension of deprivation, which in turn may generate an extra element of underachievement (cited in Young, 1984/6: p. 235).

But perhaps the main theme of the Swann Report, as reflected in its title, was that coming to terms with the polyethnic society in Britain was a task for all schools and not just those with minority pupils:

> If youngsters from the ethnic majority community leave a school with little if any understanding of the diversity of cultures and lifestyles in Britain today, and with their misunderstandings and ignorance of ethnic minority groups unchallenged or even reinforced, then there is little likelihood of the efforts of multiracial areas overcoming the climate of racism which we believe exists (cited in Young, 1984/6: p. 237).

Echoing the theme of Swann, Young went on to suggest that this implied that the potential for racism was greater in 'all-white' areas than in areas where there was a black presence. Young continued: 'inaction on the part of the former is therefore seen to be undermining any efforts being made on the part of the latter to cope with injustice'. Perhaps in view of the overall pluralist emphasis contained throughout the Swann Report, it recommended against separate schools for ethnic minorities.

Notwithstanding this recommendation, there is a long history among ethnic minority communities in Britain of self-organised supplementary or additional schools and, at the time the Swann Committee was meeting, evidence of a growing demand for separate schools altogether. Tomlinson (1985) suggested that the reasons why minority communities organised supplementary schools were complex:

> since they relate to the ways different ethnic groups wish to accommodate to the majority society, and the way this society reacts to different groups in terms of discrimination and exclusion. ... While provision ... by Asian communities may be more related to aspects of cultural diversity, and the maintenance of a cultural identity, the provision of West Indian supplementary education is most strongly connected to issues of equal opportunity (Tomlinson, 1985: pp. 66–67).

Echoing these themes, Cronin (1983/4) points to the results of a survey among teachers in supplementary schools which highlighted the importance of mother-tongue teaching:

> The responses convey the feeling that these people did not see themselves as an integral part of British society. From this followed a need to maintain strong cultural boundaries for their security and identity and the security and identity of their children. The establishment of mother-tongue schools would also go some way towards protecting and insulating the children of ethnic minorities from discrimination, prejudice and covert racism (Cronin, 1983/4: p. 259).

When Tomlinson was writing there was some support among Black communities for separate Black schools, with the primary role of such schools being seen as promoting equality of opportunity by providing Black children with the possibility of gaining the credentials necessary to succeed in the labour market. Among Muslims, on the other hand,

Tomlinson suggested that the main motivations were for mother-tongue teaching, and the transmission of religious and cultural values. Tomlinson suggested that for many years schools were unreceptive to the concerns of Muslim parents and it was this reticence that fuelled the demand for separate or supplementary provision. However, Tomlinson added that:

> ...there are some signs that in Bradford, and elsewhere, the need for separate schooling is seen as less important now that state schools are beginning to take account of Muslim cultural, religious and dietary needs (Tomlinson, 1985: p. 73).

What Tomlinson could not foresee, however, was the consequences of the publication of Salman Rushdie's novel, The Satanic Verses, in 1988, and the 'fatwa' issued by Ayatollah Khomeini that sentenced Rushdie to death in 1989. According to Dilip Hiro, the controversy created a new unity among secular and liberal Muslims, and traditionalists, which strengthened the hand of the traditionalists and, in particular, enhanced the drive for separate Islamic schools:

> The incomprehension of the media and the insensitivity of the government, revealed by the Satanic Verses issue, added insult to injury. In a sense, the Rushdie affair crystallized a host of Muslim grievances. 'It is about a symbolic controversy in which lots of other Muslim fears and anxieties and aspirations are tied up', stated Max Madden, Labour MP for Bradford West. 'How they believe that non-Muslims regard them; their feelings that they are unwelcome every day of their lives' (Hiro, 1992: p. 188).

Hiro contrasted the willingness of the British state to permit separate religious schools for the Church of England, Roman Catholics and Jews, with the rejection of proposals to establish voluntary-aided Muslim schools until 1989 (see also, Cumper, 1990: p. 387). Ironically, while the 1988 Education Reform Act had been criticised for restricting multiculturalist and anti-racist initiatives in education (Troyna, 1990; Taylor, 1990; Hardy and Vieler-Porter, 1992) or promoting a fictive national homogeneity (Gilroy, 1992), it provided, through the opting-out procedure, a mechanism whereby separate Muslim schools could occur (Cumper, 1990: p. 387; Hiro, 1992: p. 313). This was so not least because of the already existing *de facto* segregation that existed in many urban schools (Tomlinson, 1985: 70; Cumper, 1990: p. 384), a pattern evident also in many inner-city schools in the US (Kozol, 1992: p. 45).

Throughout this period the impetus towards pluralism in education that had been built up over the previous two decades slowly, but surely, dissipated. The Rampton/Swann enquiry may have been the last hurrah of the last 1970s Labour government, but the reports were published during the terms of Conservative governments that had demonstrably little interest in educational interventions for the achievement of social goals. In truth, for some years the Conservatives appeared to have no strategic plan for what they wanted to do with the education system, or rather, factions within the party offered different strategic directions without any particular one gaining ascendancy (Timmins, 1996).

This was to change with the passage of the 1988 Education Reform Act. This represented the most significant educational legislation since 1947 and provided for a fundamental shift in priority. The core feature of the reform was the introduction of a market orientation to schools. Parents were given greater choice over their children's schools. In order to inform parental choice, more information on schools was provided than at any time in the past, including school performance levels and inspection reports. Schools in turn were given greater financial and administrative responsibility in order that they could initiate measures that would lead to higher performance, hence making them more popular in the market-place. In order to encourage the schools to seek pupils, arrangements for funding were changed towards a per pupil basis. The absent presence in this discussion is the Local Education Authority (LEA) which had hitherto controlled and administered schools. In fact the reform measures consciously reduced the power and authority of LEAs. In the new system some power and authority was devolved to schools, and some was appropriated to central government in order that it could provide the overall context within which the market would operate.

One example of the new central authority could be seen in the other major consequence of the Education Reform Act, that is the establishment of a statutory National Curriculum. In the pre-reform period the curriculum was largely the responsibility of schools and teachers, with advice normally being provided by LEAs. The National Curriculum, by contrast, included details of the amount of time that was to be assigned to specific curriculum areas, each of which had a specified content of study and defined attainment targets which were to be measured by a national system of testing. Additional measures followed in the years afterwards, but for the present purposes the most significant lay in changes that provided for parental choice and hence, gave popular and over-subscribed schools the ability to choose among applicants. To some this made it easier for schools to introduce selection by ability, either directly or indirectly, and fuelled a continuing concern that a hidden agenda towards the general reintroduction of a selective system of grammar and secondary was in operation (Benn and Chitty, 1996).

In the initial aftermath of these reforms perhaps the most notable feature was the apparent neglect of any issues related to ethnic pluralism in the new National Curriculum. To the extent that such issues featured at all in the curriculum documents, they appeared to be little more than add-ons and this despite the accumulated body of curricular experience that had been developed over previous years. Another issue to arise at these early stages concerned a debate over the content of the history curriculum and, more particularly, the extent to which this constructed a mono-cultural account of Britain's past (Nash et al., 2000).

Ironically this was also the period when the extent of information on the ethnic diversity of Britain was perhaps higher than at any time in the past due to data available from the 1991 Census of Population. This revealed that three million people were members of ethnic minorities in Britain, constituting over five per cent of the population. The three largest minority communities were people of Indian descent (28 per cent of all minorities), people of African-Caribbean descent (17 per cent) and people of Pakistani descent (16 per cent). It should be noted that over half of African-Caribbeans had been born in Britain. The other minority communities included Black Africans (7 per cent), other Blacks (6 per cent), Bangladeshis (5 per cent), Chinese (5 per cent) and other Asians (7 per cent). The minorities were differentially distributed across Britain with the largest concentrations to be found in London and the South East, and the industrialised urban centres of the West Midlands. The Census data revealed also that African-Caribbeans had a rate of unemployment that was almost twice that of the White community, while the rates for Black Africans was three times that of Whites, and for Bangladeshis it was three and a half times the rate for Whites.

A general assessment of the impact of the education reforms was provided by Tomlinson (1997). She began by reminding us of the period when schools in Britain consciously moved towards greater accommodation of ethic minorities and some indication of improved levels of performance of ethnic minority children were being identified. In assessing the effect of the reforms, Tomlinson asked four questions: first, was it of any consequence that ethnic minorities in Britain were, as we have seen above, disproportionately located in urban contexts and in lower socioeconomic groups? Second, what was the impact of the new education market on ethnic segregation? Third, what was the effect of reducing the power and authority of LEAs? And fourth, was there any evidence of tangible gains in the educational opportunities available to ethnic minorities as a consequence of the changes in education?

Comparative evidence on school choice systems suggests that higher social groups are more likely to gain, perhaps because they are better able to use the choice procedures to their advantage, or more simply because they are more likely to use these procedures (OECD, 1994; Cohn, 1997). Similar patterns have been found in studies of choice mechanisms in Britain (Ball et al., 1994; 1997), implying that ethnic minorities would be disadvantaged. This disadvantage would appear to be compounded by the disproportionate location of ethnic minorities in urban contexts, as it is urban schools that are most likely to suffer negative consequences of choice, including falling rolls and funds (Audit Commission, 1996).

As to the second question, Tomlinson concluded that the introduction of an education market made it likely that ethnic segregation would be enhanced rather than reduced. This was so because, once the reform legislation was passed, it became quickly evident that some White parents sought to exercise their new-found right to choose one school over another on the basis that the preferred school had a lower proportion of ethnic minority pupils on its roll. Furthermore, parental choice was privileged over the anti-discrimination provisions of the Race Relations Acts.

The earlier part of this chapter examined the development of curriculum initiatives aimed at promoting pluralism in schools. Many of these initiatives were supported and encouraged through the LEAs and LEA advisors. Clearly, therefore, a reduction in the role and authority of LEAs would be likely to have an immediate impact on curricular support, quite apart from the reduced priority attached to plural issues in the statutory curriculum, as noted above. An additional factor lay in budget devolution to schools in which LEAs were very limited in the extent to which they could skew funds for social ends. Furthermore, Tomlinson suggested that while the money going to schools carried with it the implication of greater decision-making on their part, in practice the degree of flexibility available in the budget was very limited, thus reducing still further the potential for new school-based initiatives.

Was Tomlinson able to identify any gains for ethnic minorities as a consequence of the reforms? Her conclusion was that any gains were very limited and partial. There was some evidence, she suggested, that Muslim parents had become more ambitious for the education of the daughters, and that middle-class Blacks and Asians were able to enjoy some of the benefits derived from parental choice by their White peers. In general, however, Tomlinson concluded that the disadvantages outweighed the advantages. Their social position made the minorities more likely to suffer disadvantage from the outworking of the reform measures, while the absence of any race-conscious elements within the reforms allowed for indirect procedures to operate against them.

Towards the end of the 1990s more data began to emerge on the educational experience of minority communities, partly due to the increasing amount of data in the public domain and partly, perhaps, due to the ever-increasing likelihood of a change in government. The Office for Standards in Education (OFSTED) commissioned a review of research evidence on the experience of ethnic minorities in Britain, thereby providing the most comprehensive picture since the 1985 Swann Report. When examining attainment patterns Gilborn and Gipps (1996) showed the diversity that existed across the minority communities. Thus, in 1994 approximately 45 per cent of White 16 year olds achieved five or more GCSEs at grade C or above. This figure was equalled or exceeded by Indian, Chinese and some other Asian groups, while a much lower proportion of Black and Bangladeshi children achieved this criterion. Despite this attainment difference, however, a higher proportion of minorities tended to stay in post-compulsory education than Whites, perhaps because of a perceived need to gain credentials in order to compete in the labour market (see also MacKinnon et al., 1995; Karn, 1997).

Gilborn and Gipps (1996) also reviewed qualitative evidence of the experience on minority children in schools. This indicated that while some minority pupils experienced racial harassment, the extent and nature of this problem was often not recognised by their teachers. Asian pupils, in particular, seemed to fall into this situation. African-Caribbean pupils were between three and six times more likely to be excluded from school in comparison with White pupils (see also Social Exclusion Unit, 1998), a pattern which held for boys and girls, and for pupils in primary and secondary education. The research evidence suggested that there was a problem of conflict between White teachers and African-Caribbean pupils. Ironically, while White teachers held more positive attitudes towards Asian pupils, at times this could also descend into simplistic patronising stereotypes, especially in their views of Asian girls. Overall, then, the review by Gilborn and Gipps (1996) indicated a series of issues and problems that remained tangible during the years of the Conservative governments, even though they remained largely outside the realm of policy interest.

The election of the new Labour government under Tony Blair in 1997 caused some to think that equality and race issues would be given a renewed priority. In one area there certainly was fairly rapid change: this was the issue of public funding for separate schools for minority communities, an issue that had been considered and rejected by the Swann Committee, as discussed above. As early as 1986 the Islamia school in London had applied for public funding. This initial application was rejected in 1990, went to judicial review in 1992 and rejected again in 1993 on the basis that there were surplus places in schools in the area already. In the mid-1990s Islamic schools in Birmingham, and Islamia school, attempted to gain Grant Maintained status as Islamic schools. In 1997 formal proposals to this end were published and in 1998 the new Labour Minister of Education approved the proposals. The Grant Maintained category of schools was to disappear under the Labour government, but the principle of public funding of separate ethnic minority schools was now unambiguously established. This was reinforced by the announcement of public funding for a Sikh school in February 1999. There was not, however, a sudden growth in the number of these schools: by January 2003 while there were over 14,000 primary and secondary schools in receipt of public funds in England, only 41 of these were run by denominational authorities that were not Christian, and of these 33 were run by Jewish communities. Apart from the Christian and Jewish schools, the denominational schools in England accommodated less than 0.02 per cent of pupils overall, while in the schools system as a whole 14 per cent of pupils above compulsory school age were classified as belonging to a non-White ethnic group, while 11 per cent of primary pupils and 9 per cent of secondary pupils had a first language other than English (DFES, 2003).

Notwithstanding these developments, however, the priority for the new Labour Minister in education was in raising standards, promoting action on key skills such as literacy and numeracy, and targeting resources on specific areas of education such as early years provision and lifelong learning. Despite the claim that this priority included the inclusive goal of extending raised standards to minorities and others, and thereby reducing the historically wide variance in educational outcomes, this set of priorities led some to complain that new Labour differed little in its educational policy from the Conservatives. More particularly, many criticised the policy on the grounds that it remained largely blind to issues of race in schools (Hatcher, 1997; Gilborn, 1997).

The 'third way' advocated by Tony Blair disavowed the traditional Labour approach of using the state to reorient social institutions in new directions and, it was hoped, thereby achieve defined social goals. Rather, the new claim was that policy had to be judged largely on its effectiveness in meeting those goals, and almost any tactic could legitimately be used towards that end. This included the use of private sector techniques and partners, alongside public institutions. All of this offered a Rawlsian compromise – rather than a variant of the neo-liberal 'trickle-down' approach advocated by previous Conservative governments – which attempted to use the dynamism of the market while attempting to contain economic and other inequalities within set limits. If society benefited from this new pragmatism, then so too would the ethnic minorities. Thus, educational policy was largely driven by economic priorities, but leavened by some degree of a commitment to social justice. However, policy towards minority issues was to achieve a special priority due to two separate events. The first of these followed the murder of the Black teenager Stephen Lawrence, which dramatically pushed the issue of race to the front of the policy agenda. This was only reinforced by a series of bungled investigations by the Metropolitan Police into the murder and unsuccessful attempts to prosecute the alleged perpetrators, following which a committee was established under Sir William MacPherson to examine what had happened. The second event concerned a series of riots in cities of Northern England in Summer 2001, most especially because they revealed a wide level of *de facto* racial segregation in housing and education.

The MacPherson Report (1999) revealed an extraordinary lack of action and concern by the police authorities in investigating the murder of Stephen Lawrence and attributed this to 'institutional racism' within the police service. The Report offered a series of recommendations on how this might be addressed and included some specific recommendations for initiatives in education. Thus, it recommended that the National Curriculum should be amended to include more recognition of the cultural diversity of British society and more overt action to combat racism. Schools should be given a duty to implement anti-racist measures. This should include a commitment to record racist incidents in school and to report this information to pupils, parents, governors and the LEA. The report also recommended that schools should publish annual data on the number of racist incidents on their premises and information on the number of exclusions disaggregated by race. Furthermore, it was recommended that school inspectors should assess the implementation of these measures.

OFSTED (1999) provided a follow-up to the recommendations of Gilborn and Gipps (1996) and found that while levels of achievement were rising generally, not all ethnic minorities seemed to share in this improvement. More important, while a majority of schools were engaged in initiatives to improve provision and raise attainment, few schools monitored these initiatives in a systematic way and they rarely included a specific focus on ethnic minority pupils. Secondary schools tended to be better at analysing attainment data by ethnic group, but few linked this analysis into their policy for raising attainment. In a similar vein, although most schools had equal opportunities policies, few had procedures for monitoring their implementation and there was little evidence that they impacted on practice. Furthermore, OFSTED (1999) found little evidence that many schools reviewed their curricular or pastoral strategies to ensure that they reflected the needs and interests of ethnic minority pupils. If there was institutional racism in English schools, in other words, there appeared to be little evidence that effective measures were being taken to roll it back. Further follow-up work on this theme was provided by Gilborn and Mirza (2000) who argued for the centrality of policy on ethnic minorities to education:

> If any individual is denied the opportunity to fulfil their potential because of their racial, ethnic, class or gendered status it is now widely understood that society as a whole bears a social and economic cost by being deprived of the fruits of their enterprise, energy and imagination (Gilborn and Mirza, 2000: p. 6).

They highlighted once more the complex patterns of attainment within and between ethnic minority groups, but argued that distinct patterns of inequality remained, particularly for African-Caribbean, Pakistani and Bangladeshi young people, and that there was even some evidence of increasing inequalities. In reviewing a series of studies which attempted to identify factors which could contribute to higher attainment, they suggested that significant factors should include clear commitment and leadership from school principals and LEAs, an inclusive strategy which included pupil and community perspectives, efforts to enhance awareness of the importance of ethnic minority issues among teachers and others, openness in identifying the way ethnic status mediated practice in school and a clear commitment to high expectations and standards. There existed an inclusive priority at a national level, but their review suggested that this was more rhetorical then real, to the extent that there was limited evidence of a consistently understood or applied translation of this policy at local authority level. These conclusions were only reinforced by a series of other reports published at around the same time (Fitzgerald et al., 2000; Owen et al., 2000; Pathak, 2000).

Similar themes emerged from an independent assessment of race relations in Britain initiated by the Runnymeade Trust (Parekh Report, 2000). The report argued that Britain had reached a significant turning point at which:

> Neither equality nor respect for difference is a sufficient value on its own. The two must be held together, mutually challenging and supportive. (Parekh Report, 2000: p. 105).

The challenge, they argued, was to re-imagine Britain's past and future identity, balance equality and difference, and confront and eliminate racism. In addition, these goals had to be pursued by reducing material inequalities and establish a human rights culture. In education, their prescription was very similar to the factors identified above, including more effective use of monitoring, raising awareness, altering the curriculum, and adopting more inclusive processes for engaging with pupils and communities. In addition, they argued for a more explicit incorporation of equity considerations in teacher education and for a new priority for these issues generally to be highlighted through the school inspection system.

Whether the end of the twentieth century was a crucial turning-point in the history of race relations in Britain might have been argued at the time, but the year after the Parekh Report was published offered one vision of a possible future. In the Spring and Summer of 2001 riots broke out across a number of cities in Northern England. Whatever the immediate spark for the violence, it seemed very quickly to take on a racial character, with tension in particular between Asian and White youth. In the aftermath of these events a number of cities, including Burnley, Bradford and Oldham, established enquiry teams to examine the causes and circumstances of the violence (Clarke, 2001; Ouseley, 2001; Ritchie, 2001)). In addition, the Home Office established an enquiry team to visit all the affected cities and a number of other towns and cities of Northern England that had not been affected by violence (Cantle, 2001).

Despite differences in details, the conclusions of these various investigations highlighted a range of common factors. Thus, they identified a high level of residential segregation in many of the towns and this then had created a high level of *de facto* segregation in schools. The cities were often affected also by economic decline, the collapse of traditional industries and high levels of social disadvantage. Segregation between the communities seems to have constrained contact and understanding between them, but this allied with the effects of social and economic disadvantage, had fuelled resentment that some communities were receiving more help than others. In particular, this view seems to have been widely held by Whites in the areas and this perspective was both fuelled and exploited by far-right political organisations. Some of the investigators were shocked by a level of 'casual racism' they found among Whites, but there were also divisions and tensions between different Asian communities.

To a large extent the reports also identified a common way forward, based on the importance of dealing positively with diversity and finding ways of creating more cohesive and interconnected communities. They identified a key role for schools in promoting positive citizenship values, recognising both rights and responsibilities, and suggested that schools ought to explore ways of achieving more racially balanced intakes. All of this was to be part of wider, coordinated local strategies for community cohesion. The history of race relations in Britain from the Second World War onwards is based on an attempt to create a settled, integrated society, albeit that the basis for integration has changed dramatically over time. Sometimes this has been based on fictive notions of British homogeneity, while at other times it has recognised the value of difference and struggled to acknowledge the changing nature of Britishness itself. That the twenty-first century opened with riots between White and Asian youth in towns and cities of Northern England is testament to how difficult this task is and how much more still needs to be achieved.

8
From Apartheid to Democracy: Education in South Africa

Introduction

The previous chapters focused on countries where education had been used as a means of integrating societies. Indeed, one of the critiques of the traditional assimilationist approaches had been precisely because they had refused to give due regard to the actual diversity that existed within society. Thus, one of the consequences of this critique was to shift educational policy in the US and Britain away from a homogenising role towards one where schools attempted to reflect diverse interests and identities within their respective societies. Broadly speaking the shift was towards a pluralist education approach in that it recognised the need to deal with the actual plural nature of society. However, the preferred approach in both places was to adopt a version of pluralism which sought variation within schools rather than between them. In other words, the intention was that each school should reflect the pluralism of the wider society. As can be seen in both contexts, however, the achievement of this goal is problematic and some have argued that it is, in fact, not achievable. From this perspective some have argued in favour of institutional pluralism, that is, in favour of a plurality of schools within which minorities of all kinds can operate their own schools in order to maintain some degree of cultural identity and continuity. This view of pluralism involves the establishment of variation between schools, rather than necessarily within them. It is to examples of this type of approach we now turn, as we look at school systems that are based on separate provision for different communities.

The two examples we will consider are apartheid South Africa and Northern Ireland. Under the apartheid regime, South Africa embodied institutional segregation for Blacks and Whites and this extended to education even after other forms of segregation had been removed. After the establishment of democracy this institutional racism was dismantled, but, inevitably, achieving a level playing field has been slow and fraught with difficulty. Northern Ireland has operated *de facto* separate schools for Protestants and Catholics since the formation of the state in 1921/22, but many within and without Northern Ireland wonder why this is maintained, especially now that a tenuous peace agreement is in place. This chapter will examine the development of apartheid in South Africa and its implementation through education. It will then go on to examine briefly how the system changed as South Africa moved towards democracy in the 1990s and consider the prospects for the future. The next chapter will focus on Northern Ireland and its story.

Historical background

Before the arrival of Europeans, Khoisan-speaking bushmen and Bantu-speaking agriculturalists co-existed in the territory that was to become South Africa. Initially Europeans used the Cape of Good Hope as a resting point in travels further east, but later Dutch settlers developed into a self-supporting community of farmers who expanded inland and clashed with the indigenous communities. These Afrikaners established independent Boer Republics at the end of the eighteenth century, although they were short-lived as British Imperial authority was imposed on the territory as a whole. British rule added another community to the ethnic mix as Asian workers were imported from India, as had occurred in others parts of the Empire (Davenport and Saunders, 2000).

Slavery had been abolished throughout the British Empire, but the Boer farmers clung to an interpretation of the Bible which claimed that all Africans, the 'sons of Ham', had been appointed by God as their slaves (Davidson, 1985: pp. 256–257). The early years of the nineteenth century saw numerous wars between, inter alia, the British, Boers and Africans, and the Boers shifted ever further into the interior to escape British authority. When the British decided to formally abolish slavery in 1834 the Boers embarked on their 'Great Trek' across the Orange and Fish rivers into their new 'promised land'. This journey and their pastoralist orientation combined to form the national story of the Boer community. The fact that they had overcome African opposition and resisted British authority provided self-confirmation of the sacred status of their community (Pakenham, 1982). In time, of course, the key to South Africa came to be based on its enormous mineral wealth and it was upon this resource that the country developed.

The development of apartheid

Racism among the Boers had its origins in a religious discourse and, in the twentieth century, this quasi-theological justification remained potent, with added elements from the biological essentialism that had developed in Europe. In 1935 Nico Diederichs, who was later to become State President of South Africa, justified separate development in the following manner:

> God willed that ... at the human level, there should be a multiplicity and diversity of nations, languages and cultures and just as it would be a violation of God's natural law to try to reduce all colours to one colour and all sounds to one sound, everything in nature to one dull monotony so it is just as much of a desecration of His law to destroy the multiplicity of nations in the world for the sake of a monochromatic, monotonous and monolithic humanity.

Diederichs, like other Afrikaner intellectuals at the time, looked to Nazi Germany for inspiration. Unlike the older Afrikaner elite who held Africans as an inferior community within a common society, Diederichs and his peers looked to the possibility of an exclusively White society (Stent, 1994: p. 53). An opportunity to implement this vision was provided at the 1948 election after which the National Party, the political voice of the Afrikaners, headed a coalition government. They quickly set about establishing a legal and institutional infrastructure to create separate development for Blacks and Whites. They began by restricting the voting rights of Black Africans, then introduced a series of laws which separated the communities in various domains of life, until they had established their grand vision of apartheid.

The nature of the process can be discerned from a quick review of the main planks of apartheid legislation. In 1949 the Prohibition of Mixed Marriages Act outlawed marriage between Whites and other races, and nullified mixed marriages which South Africans obtained abroad. In 1950 the Immorality Amendment Act outlawed sexual relations between Whites and other races, the Population Registration Act mandated an official codification of the entire population into race communities, the Suppression of Communism Act provided the basis for banning political activity that was hostile to the government, while the Group Areas Act allowed the government to allocate specific parts of the country to specific racial communities, thereby allowing for the physical separation of peoples. In 1952 the Pass laws were introduced so that all Black people over the age of 16 years had to carry an internal passport which could be demanded by the police at any time. In 1953 the Separate Amenities Act mandated the provision of separate amenities to Blacks and Whites in public areas and specifically stated that separate provision need not be equal. In the same year the Bantu Education Act laid out the framework for the curriculum of Black schools and gave authority to the Minister of Education to close schools which refused to adhere to these new restrictions. In 1959 the curiously misnamed Extension of University Education Act excluded all other races from White universities and established five new ethnic universities. Other legislation laid the legal basis for Bantu Homelands which were to provide a system of native self-rule across different parts of the country. The Homelands legislation also removed residency rights from the large numbers of Black workers who serviced the mines and factories in the 'White' parts of the country. Many Blacks were, in fact, forcibly moved from territory allocated to Whites or Coloureds. The grand vision of apartheid intended that the Bantu Homelands would, in time, achieve independence so that the territory of South Africa would become a melange of separate states, each providing a home base for the multiplicity of separate communities in the region.

The Homelands policy was central to the vision of apartheid in a number of respects. It tried to provide a justification for White domination by claiming that separate development was natural and fair, not least because the whole society was a collection of minorities. The provision of separate Homelands for separate African communities was an attempt to deflect and divide Black political aspirations, and encourage the development of a Black political elite in each of the Homeland areas whose political future depended on the retention of the overall system. And it allowed for a reduction in the number of Blacks who were permitted to live in 'White' areas and a draconian set of rules for the control of those who were permitted to remain.

Apartheid education

We have seen above how legislation in the 1950s had established the basis for separate Black schools. In 1963 comparable legislation provided the basis for separate Coloured schools, followed in 1965 by the establishment of separate Indian schools. In 1967 the National Education Policy Act laid the basis for Christian National Education (CNE), the defining ethos of White schooling which we will explore in a little more detail below. The rationale behind separate development in education was not simply to keep the different racial communities apart, but to locate and place their role in the wider society. Hendrik Verwoerd, who, as Native Affairs Minister, was largely responsible for constructing the edifice of apartheid, provided the lodestone for this when he said in parliament:

> I just want to remind the Honourable Members of Parliament that if the Native in South Africa is being taught to expect that he will lead his adult life under the policy of equal rights, he is making a big mistake. The native must not be subject to a school system which draws him away from his own community, and misleads him by showing him the green pastures of European society in which he is not allowed to graze. ... There is no place for [the Bantu] in the European community above the level of certain forms of labour ... For that reason it is of no avail to him to receive a training which has as its aim absorption in the European community.

The material consequences of this were clear. In 1970, for every Rand spent on the education of African children, 4 Rand were spent on the education of Coloured children, 5 Rand on the education of Indian children and 17 Rand on the education of White children. Whereas the teacher-pupil ratio in White schools was 1:20, the ratio was 1:58 in African schools. The drop-out rate among African children was higher than that for Whites which meant that a higher proportion of African children tended not to take their education beyond the primary level. The attainment levels of African pupils were markedly lower than the other communities, and varied quite considerably across the Homelands each of which organised its own school system. In 1970 over half the African adult population was illiterate. In 1974 there were less than 13,000 African students at university, in comparison with almost 70,000 White students. As late as 1988 almost a third of teachers in African schools had not graduated with a secondary school level qualification. Separate development in education, in other words, meant inferior provision for African pupils because the intention always had been that education would limit rather than realise their potential (Gordon et al., 1978: p. 461; Christie, 1991: pp. 101–136).

That a markedly different manifest destiny was intended for White pupils is clear also when we examine practice within their schools. As stated above, the organising principles for White education were provided by the concept of Christian National Education (CNE). The origins of CNE schools go back to the early years of this century when Afrikaners established separate schools to inculcate their own brand of Calvanism and Boer identity. At one point almost 200 CNE schools operated, but financial and other pressures meant that by 1907 few remained (Christie, 1991: p. 50). In the 1940s the CNE movement was revived and it grew steadily alongside Afrikaner nationalism. As indicated above CNE principles provided the legal basis for White schools following legislation in 1967. The schools were to have a Christian character, while recognising the particular religious adherence of pupils, and a broadly national character. This latter aspect was defined by the Ministry of Education in 1971 as the active promotion of a sense of nationalism and patriotism among pupils. Both elements were to be achieved through the curriculum and through school rituals and festivals (Christie, 1991: pp. 175–178).

In the Transvaal two special school programmes provide a particular insight into the practice of these principles. One of these was the Youth Preparedness programme, which included on its compulsory curriculum such components as emergency planning, fire fighting, drilling and marching, drilling, shooting and orchestra, shooting and self-defence, vocational guidance and moral preparedness. In case the implicit message was not explicit enough the Youth Preparedness programme was run with the aid of the army, the South African Defence Force (SADF). When this programme was launched in 1972 the Director of Education in the Transvaal claimed that it was needed due to the threats facing the South African value system. The other programme addressed moral and physical teaching through Veld schools. The point of this programme was to take White children from urban settings and bring them into a rural environment. Part of the purpose of this was to reconnect Afrikaner children to their pastoralist heritage. But the contemporary significance of the Veld school experience was unambiguous in that it sought to develop 'better' South Africans who were prepared for emergencies and aware of the threats facing the country. Furthermore, it provided an opportunity to assess the leadership potential of young people for the predicted struggle ahead (Christie, 1991: pp. 185–187).

End of apartheid

By the early 1970s the apartheid system seemed secure. South Africa was excluded officially from the corridors of most international organisations but there were few effective barriers to international trade. Furthermore, the internal opposition provided by groups like the African National Congress (ANC), the Pan African Congress (PAC) or the South African Communist Party (SACP) seemed to be dissipated and their leaders largely forgotten. It was within this context that students in Soweto, a township on the outskirts of Johannesburg, decided to go on strike in opposition to an attempt to impose Afrikaans as the medium of instruction in their schools. When the security forces arrived in the township to confront the student marchers, they opened fire and scores of children died. Hector Pedersen, the first to die, remains the iconic image of that day's tragic events. Indeed, a statue of Pedersen now stands in Soweto as a memorial to all those who died in the Student Uprising. A quarter of a decade earlier over 60 Africans had been killed by police at a PAC-organised demonstration against pass laws at Sharpeville. Unlike then, however, the 1976 Soweto school students' uprising provided a spark to more opposition, including, in 1980, a strike among African pupils in all Cape schools.

In response to the growing unrest, the government introduced new education legislation in 1979 and generally improved the position of African schools. In 1980 the De Lange Commission was established to conduct an in-depth investigation into education. Its 1981 report recommended the establishment of a single Education Department to cover all schools. While the government accepted some of the principles outlined in the De Lange report, it rejected the notion of a single Department in favour of a tripartite arrangement that fitted within the political model with which it was hoped political stability could be restored to the country, although in truth the emergent structure had the character of institutional pluralism gone mad. The first element of the reform structure in education was the maintenance of separate education departments for South Africa, the four Homelands of Transkei, Bophutatswana, Venda and Ciskei, that had achieved independence, albeit only recognised by South Africa, and the remaining six 'national' states for whom eventual independence was the preferred official future. Within South Africa the new political arrangements had established a dual system under a powerful State President. One side of the system involved a tricameral parliament to replace the old Whites-only parliament. Separate electoral rolls and chambers operated for

Whites (House of Assembly), Coloureds (House of Representatives) and Asians (House of Delegates). A Council of Ministers (Own Affairs) oversaw the work of these three Houses, and each of the Houses operated 'Own Affairs' Departments of Education and Culture. The second element of the dual system was led by a Cabinet (General Affairs) under which sat two education departments. The 'General Affairs' National Education was set up to oversee finance, teachers' salaries, teacher registration and curriculum, while the Department of Education and Training (DET) continued to look after African education. The reform structure as a whole attempted to mitigate external pressure on South Africa by according a degree of political involvement to some Black communities, and thereby also to attempt to divide internal Black opposition to apartheid. By the time it was all introduced, however, apartheid had already passed its point of survival.

The reforms as a whole were as effective in stemming the tide of opposition as King Canute had been in stemming the tide. A coalition of opposition groups, including the Trade Unions, Churches and other community and political organisations, came together to form the United Democratic Front (UDF). The UDF provided a focus for opposition to apartheid and operated a link to the ANC outside the country, but had been formed primarily to oppose the tricameral parliament on the grounds that it denied votes to Africans. In 1984 violence spread through townships leading to the declaration of a state of emergency. The level of opposition was such that key sections of the White elite began to realise that more radical change was needed and various negotiations started to take place. In 1985 some White business leaders met with ANC leaders in Zambia and the State President initiated discussions with the gaoled ANC leader Nelson Mandela. In 1986 informal contacts were opened between White political leaders and the ANC leadership abroad, and over the whole period informal contacts took place within the country between White politicians and the UDF. Not all Whites were reconciled with this process. Some members of the National Party who opposed the reformist approach broke away to form the Conservative Party, while a host of smaller, more militant, Afrikaner groups were formed to oppose change. In 1989 the National Party elected a new leader and State President, F.W. De Klerk. The pace of change now quickened with the release from gaol of some key ANC leaders, the legalisation of an ANC march in Cape Town and a face-to-face meeting between De Klerk and Mandela.

The culmination of this activity came with the release of Nelson Mandela in 1990 and the unbanning of the ANC and SACP. In response Umkhonto We Sizwe, the armed wing of the ANC, suspended its military action. The new circumstances created a public political space within which formal negotiations on the future could develop. Initially the talks were held out of the public gaze and were as much a process of familiarisation as anything else. Alongside these positive developments, however, was an escalation in township violence between rival political groups. The main violence was between supporters of the ANC and Inkatha, an ethnic Zulu party whose leader, Chief Buthelezi, had his political base in Kwazulu. The ANC suspected that Inkatha was receiving tacit support from the security forces, a suspicion that was to be confirmed some years later.

In 1991 the first formal multi-party talks opened in the Convention for a Democratic South Africa (CODESA I). This was a forum within which all political interests within South Africa, including representatives of the Homelands leaders, were represented. In an attempt to out-maneuver right-wing political opponents within his own constituency, State President De Klerk called a Whites-only referendum to endorse the negotiation route. He duly received his mandate. However, the CODESA I talks only revealed the extent of the difference between the main political actors. The ANC favoured a transition to democratic majority rule in a largely centralised state. Inkatha preferred a federalised political system which would secure its autonomy in Kwazulu. Meanwhile the National Party seemed to assume that the White minority should retain an effective veto over political developments despite being a 12 per cent minority in the population (Waldemar, 1997: pp. 191–195). The second round of talks began at CODESA II with a heightened sense of mutual antagonism. De Klerk and the National Party felt that the successful referendum result had strengthened their hand in the negotiations (Davenport, 1998). By contrast, the ANC concluded that the result had weakened the right-wing opposition and thereby reduced the need for compromise with the National Party. In an increasingly acrimonious environment the CODESA II talks eventually collapsed in May 1992.

Ironically, it would take two mass killings to restore a sense of urgency to the process and convince them that negotiation was the only practical way forward because, it would appear, these massacres discredited the extremists on both sides. Throughout the talks process there had been a steady increase in violence, with a particularly high level of conflict occurring in the Townships between supporters of the ANC and Inkatha. ANC supporters were convinced that Inkatha was being armed and encouraged by the security forces as part of a secret 'third force' strategy aimed at encouraging intra-African ethnic strife. Despite protestations to the contrary by State President De Klerk, a massacre of Township residents by an unknown faction in Boipatong served to discredit the third force.

Militant factions within the ANC sought to raise the political stakes by toppling Homelands leaders. A rally was held on the outskirts of Ciskei and despite assurances that no attempt would be made to enter the Homeland territory, a large section of the crowd was led to try exactly this. The security forces from Bisho opened fire and 29 people were killed. Just as the Biopatong massacre served to discredit the militants who were resisting change, so the Bisho massacre served to discredit militants who were trying to provoke radical change.

In response to the heightened situation created by the killings, and the fear that this was merely a foretaste of what might occur if political agreement could not be found, Joe Slovo, a leading figure in the ANC negotiating team, proposed the establishment of 'sunset clauses' which would guarantee the position of White public officials and civil servants after the transition to a democratic settlement. This seemed to break the logjam and led to agreement on arrangements for a democratic election. During 1993 a transitional council was established to oversee government until the election was held in 1994. As the election approached the level of violence increased. A particular concern held by many was the eventual stance to be taken by the more militant White groups who were opposed to the end of apartheid. A number of small political groups had coalesced round the leadership of General Viljoen, but he was embarrassed, and the opposition largely discredited, following the attempted invasion of Bophuthatswana by militant forces of the neo-Nazi AWB. The AWB had tried consistently to disrupt the talks process, but lost face and political influence, when its cadres were literally chased out of Bophutatswana by Black policemen. In April 1994, the ANC duly won the election, but with a majority that was not sufficiently large to allow it to alter the constitution unaided. In May 1994, Nelson Mandela completed the transition from political activist, guerilla leader and prisoner, when he was inaugurated as the first President of democratic South Africa.

Change within education

We have seen above the attempt to recast the administrative structure of education as part of the broader political reforms through which the White minority tried to head off more radical change. More generally apartheid South Africa provided the clearest example of a non-democratic pluralism, in that differentiation between ethnic communities was legally enforced in the public and private spheres. This malign pluralism was designed to ensure that power was held by the minority White population, while the majority African population was subject to restricted rights. The consequences of this were particularly evident in education. In 1975/76 the per capita amount spent on the education of African children was 42 Rand and the average teacher-pupil ratio in African schools was 1:52. By contrast, the per capita amount spent on the education of White children was over fifteen times greater at 644 Rand, and the average teacher-pupil ratio in White schools was 1:20 (Gordon et al., 1978: p. 461). This was also the year in which school pupils in Soweto rose in opposition to the attempt to impose Afrikaans as the language of teaching, leading to a boycott by pupils and teachers and, in time, to thousands of young Africans fleeing the country to enter training camps run by Umkhonto We Sizwe, the military arm of the ANC. In the same year some Roman Catholic schools decided to admit African pupils thereby defying the government's official prohibition on integrated education. While these schools were threatened with deregistration and closure, within a decade the practice of these 'open' private schools was legalised. This occurred within the context of apartheid however: the schools remained under the aegis of the White Department of Education and Culture, but were permitted to 'render services' to other racial groups.

In 1990 this possibility was extended to all schools, although in fact few historically White schools chose to move in the direction of desegregation (Christie, 1995: p. 48). Within two years, and as South Africa moved towards a democratic settlement, most schools were obliged to adopt an 'open' admissions policy. Even then, as Christie (1995) highlighted, only very small numbers of African were able to gain admittance to most of these schools, and few had attempted to develop diversity in their curriculum:

> If the models opened possibilities for desegregation rather than actively promoted them, the responses of the majority of schools suggest that they would have resisted desegregation had the government adopted a stronger policy (Christie, 1995: p. 52).

Indeed, the privatisation of the schools in fact removed them from the public education pool just before political transformation and was clearly an attempt to give White communities control over the extent and pace of change. The privatisation dimension is explored further by Tikley (1997) where he argues that it provided the basis for a variety of discourses, centred on rights and the protection of minorities, that were used by the White minority in order to cling to privileges in the educational sphere. In particular, Tikley (1997) points to the way in which the claim for 'autogenous' education, that is education which reflects the culture, religion and language of the child, accords a key role to parental influence in schools, as guardians of their children's cultural heritage. This claim can sit easily alongside the marketisation of schools as, at its centre, rests the notion of parental choice. In this context, of course, the discourse was being used to place the interests of individuals and a particular community above the wider collective interests of society as a whole.

The legacy of apartheid endures in education as democracy develops. Two years after the transition the matriculation results for schools showed a continuing pattern of very wide divergences, and the amount of money available for educational initiatives remained very limited: as Gilmour (2001) pointed out, there were very wide disparities across the schools in the qualifications of teachers, the level of capital expenditure, the curriculums which schools could provide and in the quality of education that could be provided. The ANC-led government faced a dilemma in trying to begin the task of reducing the gross inequalities of the apartheid period while at the same time running an economic policy that would maintain stability and, hopefully, encourage inward investment. The initial approach had been through the 1994 Reconstruction and Development Programme (RDP) which aimed to reduce inflation and use government spending to expand the economy and increase manufacturing employment. The core themes within the RDP were to meet basic needs, to develop human resources, to build the economy and to democratise the state and society (King and McGrath, 2002: p. 60). The education element of the policy was to include a single Education Department (instead of separate departments for the communities under apartheid) and to pursue a pro-active strategy to tackle the inequities inherited from apartheid. Soudien (2001) suggests that the government had set a target date of 2005 for equality in education. One of the specific educational initiatives involved an active attempt to equalise teacher-pupil ratios by a strategy of teacher redeployment.

By 1997, however, the RDP was replaced by the Growth, Employment and Redistribution policy (GEAR) which placed more emphasis on economic competitiveness (Davenport, 1998). King and McGrath

(2002) argued that although GEAR was presented initially as the operationalisation of the RDP vision, in fact it marked a shift towards a neo-liberal economic policy that prioritised export-led growth and a consequent downplaying of social programmes. Furthermore, they argued that while the RDP had been based on redistributivist principles, GEAR seemed to be based more on a 'trickle-down' approach. They went on to criticise the programme on the grounds that it was imposed rather than negotiated, that it failed to meet its own targets for employment creation and it failed to deal with some of the fundamental weaknesses in the South African economy.

At the level of detail too, there were problems. The teacher redeployment programme, which Soudien (2001) points out was in any case unpopular with teachers, had run into difficulties as there was a significantly higher level of teacher redundancies than had been planned (due in part to the pressures created by other parts of the reform agenda, according to Gilmour, 2001), with the consequence that the cost of the programme exceeded expectations. Many White teachers simply took their redundancy cheques and decamped to private schools. Also in 1997 a group of Cape schools won the right to appoint new teachers without having to accept candidates off the top of the transfer list, thereby undercutting one of the key elements of the policy. To add to the difficulties, a major curriculum programme had to be deferred because insufficient numbers of teachers were trained and prepared for its implementation although some have argued that the available training was inadequate in any case (Nakabugo and Siebörger, 2001), and schools were given the right to charge fees which acted as a brake on integration. All these setbacks occurred in a situation where major inequalities between schools and provinces remained, with schools in Black Townships and the former Homelands being the most disadvantaged. It was in these schools also that racial integration was having the least effect, despite the limited desegregation that could be seen in White, Coloured and Indian schools (Vally, 1998).

For some educational commentators the problem was that the elision from the RDP to GEAR had been accompanied by an official definition of equality that focused on access, that is input measures, rather than outcome, or output measures:

> The presence of user fees and the huge backlogs in education provision inherited from apartheid means that we still have a highly differentiated education system – both between public and private

schools, and within public schools. Greater access, then, has not resulted in qualitative improvement (Motala, 2001: p. 64)

In her discussion of the broader reform agenda, Motala went on to suggest that recent practice has incorporated ideas from the effective schools movements and attempted to focus attention on internal school factors which would improve the quality of teaching and learning. Of course, as Motala points out, a potential problem with this is that it might focus attention too narrowly on a limited set of indicators and hence narrow conceptualisations on the purpose of education:

> In order to broaden our notions of appropriate outcomes, it is necessary to move away from the distinction between good and bad schools, and to create a more nuanced understanding of the overall purpose of schools and of the values they are promoting. A tension continues between education for the purpose of serving the global economy and local economic growth, and education which services the broader goals of citizenship and democracy (Motala, 2001: p. 74)

The millennial edition of the South Africa Survey (Forgey et al., 1999) provided a statistical picture on the extent to which progressive change had been achieved and the continuing legacy of apartheid. Overall one-in-five of the population aged 20 years and over had no education and 44 per cent had not received any education beyond the primary level. There were wide differences between the racial groups, with 52 per cent of Africans receiving no education beyond primary level, in comparison with 2 per cent of Whites. In addition, 36 per cent of adults were illiterate. For those who did receive post-primary education the pass rate at senior certificate had declined in the years after democracy and in at least one province the data has had to be adjusted downwards due to suspected tampering. That said, as South Africa approached the millennium there was some evidence that the tide might have been turned with slight increases in the senior certificate pass rate. The goal of achieving integrated education was proceeding slowly, with only 28 per cent of all schools being defined as multiracial. Furthermore, there was a marked increase in the number of independent schools being opened.

We began this chapter by asking the question on whether the goal of a pluralist education could be achieved by recreating schools as plural institutions and by noting the limited extent to which this ideal had actually been achieved in countries such as the US and Britain. In response some have argued for institutional pluralism, that is a system of schools in which different communities have the right to run their own institutions to the extent that there might be more differences between schools than within them. The case of apartheid South Africa stands as a stark warning against an overly simplistic acceptance of the argument for institutional pluralism. Apartheid was based on the reification of difference in order to justify separation and legitimise domination. Furthermore, the consequences of this system endure in the massive and continuing inequalities that exist within South African society, while the priorities of economic development limit the extent to which action can be taken to address these inequalities. Some have felt that the ANC government would begin to lose support if there was no tangible evidence of the legacies of apartheid being reduced. It is clear that, in education at least, dealing with the consequences of the apartheid system has been a slow and difficult task. Despite this, there is little evidence that political support for the ANC government has declined or that there is popular frustration with the approach they have adopted.

One characteristic of the case of apartheid South Africa is that educational separation was forced as part of a wider political system designed to secure the domination of the White majority. Minority Rights Group (MRG) (1994) has argued that the right to separate schools for minorities is compatible with international standards on human rights, but that an important distinction needs to be drawn between those situations where separate schools are imposed, which MRG defines as segregation, and those situations where separate schools are adopted as a matter of choice. It is therefore possible that institutional pluralism may have more benign consequences in situations where minorities opt for separate schools as a matter of choice. The case of denominational schools in Northern Ireland provides an example of this form of institutional pluralism and it is to this example we turn in the next chapter.

9
Community Relations and Education in Northern Ireland

Introduction

During part of the 1990s the peace processes in Northern Ireland, South Africa and the Middle East all seemed to be following a common trajectory although, as we know, they have achieved varying levels of success and failure. Wright (1987) provided one of the best comparative books using Northern Ireland, but sadly Wright died prematurely. In the first of the Frank Wright Memorial lectures in Queen's University Belfast, Guelke examined the processes in each context and identified a key turning point when a hitherto stable situation appeared amenable to change. In South Africa the turning point came with the 1976 uprising of school students in Soweto and the killing of Hector Petersen by South African security forces. Following these events many young people fled South Africa to enter the camps of Umkhonto We Sizwe, while within South Africa a new internal opposition movement started to form. In the Middle East it was an accident in the Gaza Strip when an Israeli truck crashed into a car of Palestinian labourers, killing four and injuring the others. This was to light a spark that led to the Intifada. And Guelke pointed also to a key turning point in Northern Ireland in October 1968 when a Civil Rights march in Derry (or Londonderry) was banned by the Unionist government and attacked by the police in full view of television cameras. Given the level of violence which Northern Ireland has experienced since 1968, the events then seem extraordinarily restrained in hindsight. But at the time they had an enormous impact on perceptions.

In many respects it was perhaps appropriate that the turning point in Northern Ireland occurred in Derry/Londonderry. The political arrangements in the city were generally cited as the most blatant example of Unionist domination. A system of gerrymandered electoral wards ensured that Unionist politicians held a majority on the local council, even though the Unionist electorate comprised a minority of the city's population. It is not surprising that, to Nationalists, the city was known as the 'capital city of discrimination'. But the city had a key historical significance for Unionists also: in 1689 the Protestant inhabitants of the old city held fast against the army of Catholic King James, in support of William of Orange. There is a continuing tradition whereby a Protestant society, the Apprentice Boys, march around the walls of the old city in commemoration of the siege. In 1969 Catholic opposition to the march led to widespread rioting in the city, the virtual collapse of the police force and the introduction of British army troops to restore order. Subsequently, the city was to become a strong centre for the IRA and, indeed, parts of the city virtually ceded for a time from Northern Ireland.

A visitor to the city would now find a very different picture. Much of the city centre has been rebuilt and/or redeveloped. The city council is now unambiguously under the control of Nationalist politicians and, indeed, the most significant political contest is between the moderate Nationalist party, the SDLP, and the more radical Sinn Fein. The city appears wealthier, more settled and politically less fraught, certainly in comparison with Belfast. Despite its position as a crucible of violence in the early years of the conflict, the city was spared much of the worst of the sectarian violence as the various paramilitary groups in the city appeared to operate a *modus vivendi* that eschewed random assassinations.

But in some respects an important part of the heart of the city has gone. The River Foyle divides the city in half but its significance has become as much religious as geographic. There has been a steady and continuing decline in the Protestant population of the western part of the city. Only one small and declining area within the old city walls remains. There are a number of 'Protestant' schools on the western side, but some have become *de facto* Catholic schools, while others have a questionable future of any kind. In a very real sense, Protestants appear to have given up on that part of the city, feeling that they now count for nothing. It is as if the carefully crafted domination of the old Unionist regime has been replaced by a casual, almost careless domination by Nationalist politicians. The old system was wrong and had to be changed, because it represented the illegitimate domination of a majority by a minority. But in the changing, have we created a situation where all that had changed is the balance of power, but what remains in place is the domination of one group over another? If so, there is still no accommodation, no reconciliation with difference, no celebration of diversity.

Many plural contexts involve majority-minority relations in which the minority (or minorities) represent relatively small proportions of the population. In other circumstances, such as apartheid South Africa, power is exercised by groups that are numerically a minority. Northern Ireland represents a slightly different case in that a key part of the dynamic there lies in the closer balance of population between the two main communities, the fact that the minority maintained control over some social institutions and in a context where the population, and hence political, balance has narrowed over time. The question raised by this example, and alluded to in the illustration from Derry/ Londonderry above, is whether two groups in such a relationship can find the basis for a shared future, or whether they are fated to remain apart and in a relationship that is, at best, an uneasy co-existence. This question is perhaps particularly pertinent in education since, as we will see below, Northern Ireland has parallel school systems for Protestants and Catholics, and a relatively new, but still small, third track of integrated schools. Is it possible for a plurality of schools such as this to make a positive contribution to the promotion of tolerance and reconciliation, especially in a society that is emerging from a quarter century of violent conflict, or must institutional pluralism create barely penetrable barriers? These are the issues to be explored in this chapter.

Background to education in Northern Ireland

Mass education in Ireland has its origins in the decision to develop a national system of elementary schools in the 1830s at a time when the whole island was in the United Kingdom. The official aspiration at the time was that common schools for pupils aged 5 to 14 years would develop across the island and pupils of all denominations would attend the schools. In fact, the various Churches were able to exert sufficient influence so that, by the end of the nineteenth century, almost all schools were managed by denominational interests and were attended almost exclusively by pupils from one faith community (Akenson, 1970).

In 1921/22 Ireland was partitioned and two parliaments were established in Dublin and Belfast. The Dublin parliament represented the majority of the island in which the population was overwhelmingly Catholic and Nationalist. The Belfast parliament represented the north-east sector of the island which had a Protestant majority. Both parliaments were given the option of remaining in the United Kingdom or seeking independence: the Dublin parliament decided for independence and a route that would eventually lead to the formation of the Republic of Ireland, while the Belfast parliament opted to remain, as a self-governing region now called Northern Ireland, within the United Kingdom. The use of partition to address ethnic conflicts was widely used in the post-Versailles period and was aimed at creating more ethnically homogeneous territory. This was the motivation in Ireland as well, but in order to create a Northern Ireland territory that was economically viable it was deemed necessary to include a Catholic minority that comprised about a third of the population. The Catholic minority was predominantly Nationalist in sentiment and continued to look to the rest of Ireland for its national and political identity. This encouraged a defensiveness among the Protestant majority in Northern Ireland and discouraged them for considering political accommodation with what was seen as a potential 'fifth column'. And so the political fault-lines came to be drawn around religion, and so it remains.

Following the formation of the Northern Ireland state in 1921/22 a committee was established under Robert Lynn to consider the future organisation of schools as the existing system of national schools left most in the hands of religious authorities. The Lynn report (1922/23) recommended the establishment of three types of schools which would be differentiated by the level of public representation on their school committees and the level of public grant they received: the more of the former was matched by more of the latter. The assumption was that most of the Protestant-owned schools would transfer to public ownership as 'county' schools and receive 100 per cent funding. Most Catholic schools were expected to take the 'voluntary' option, with no public representation on the committees and limited public grant. However the hope remained that the Catholic authorities might, in time, consider the third possibility whereby there would be one-third public representation on their committees and higher grant levels than voluntary schools.

In the event the Catholic authorities choose to remain at a distance from the new Ministry of Education. More surprisingly, hardly any Protestant-owned schools transferred to 'county' school status. A campaign against the Lynn recommendations charged him with seeking to establish secular schools. The reasons for this was that the Minister of Education, Lord Londonderry, was interested in trying to provide a basis for schools in which all denominations would feel welcome. Specifically, Londonderry wanted to place religious instruction outside the normal school curriculum. Although clergy were to be permitted to come into the schools to teach their adherents, this was only to occur outside normal school hours.

This was one of the measures opposed by the Protestant Churches as they wanted Bible teaching to be a compulsory part of the curriculum for 'county' schools. Furthermore, they sought to have local control over teacher appointments, ostensibly to ensure that there would always be sufficient Protestant teachers in 'county' schools to provide proper Bible teaching. This opposition was carried out overtly and covertly through the various political and religious networks of Ulster Unionism. Londonderry's intentions were set aside and a series of amendments in the 1930s conceded most of the Protestant demands (Buckland, 1979). Thus, Bible teaching became the only statutory part of the curriculum for 'county' schools, local interests had an effective right of veto over teacher appointments, thereby largely ensuring that only Protestant teachers were appointed to these schools, and the Protestant Churches that had transferred the schools were given guaranteed positions on the new 'county' school committees. Thus, by the end of the 1930s parallel systems of Catholic and *de facto* Protestant schools were established (Dunn, 1990). This situation remained intact into the 1960s at which time government statistics indicated that 98 per cent of Catholic pupils were in 'voluntary' schools and 96 per cent of Protestant pupils were in 'county' schools (Akenson, 1973).

It was not until 1968 that a rapprochement was achieved between the Catholic authorities and the state over schools. Under this deal Catholic schools accepted public representation on their school committees, for which they received an extra level of grant. In a *quid pro quo* the arrangements for 'county' schools were changed also. They were renamed as controlled schools, under the ownership of education and library boards, but any new ones were treated as if they had been transferred. The main consequence of this was that the Protestant Churches were given automatic membership rights on the school committees of all new controlled schools. Arguably, the outcome was to reinforce the institutional separation of the schools.

By 2001 this pattern of sectarian division in schools remained as potent as ever, with the important difference that a new sector of religiously integrated schools has developed from 1981 onwards (Table 9.1). The genesis and development of the integrated schools will be examined below, but for the moment Table 9.1 illustrates the

Table 9.1   Pupils in primary, secondary and grammar schools, 2001/02 by religion and school type (numbers, and percentages by school type and by religion) (source: Department of Education statistical press release 30 April 2002)

	Catholic	Protestant & Other	Not recorded	Total
Protestant schools	7,276	135,994	14,531	157,801
Catholic schools	151,905	1,368	356	153,629
Integrated schools	5,901	7,367	1,358	14,626
All schools	165,082	144,729	16,245	326,056
Protestant schools (%)	5	86	9	100
Catholic schools (%)	99	1	0	100
Integrated schools (%)	40	50	9	99
All schools (%)	51	44	5	100
Protestant schools (%)	4	94	89	48
Catholic schools (%)	92	1	2	47
Integrated schools (%)	4	5	8	4
All schools (%)	100	100	100	100

Note: Not all columns sum up to 100 due to rounding errors.

continuing significance of religious differences across schools in general. Table 9.1 shows that Catholics comprise only five per cent of pupils in 'Protestant' schools, while Protestants comprise only one per cent of pupils in 'Catholic' schools. Overall the religious composition of pupils in the integrated schools broadly reflects the overall population proportions, but we can see that only four per cent of pupils overall attend integrated schools.

Education and the conflict

This was the situation that pertained in education when violence erupted on Northern Ireland streets in the latter part of the 1960s, followed closely by the arrival of British troops, the launch of the IRA campaign and, subsequently, the campaign by Loyalist paramilitary groups. Northern Ireland had been a fairly peaceful society prior to this: in the 1960s the average number of murders per year was in single figures, but within a few years of the outbreak of violence in one year the death toll amounted to almost 500. Not surprisingly many people looked to the segregated education system and asked whether it had contributed to community division and was helping to reproduce conflict and, on that basis, some argued that the solution lay in the development of new integrated schools (Heskin, 1980; Fraser, 1973;

Darby and Dunn, 1987). Some of the early expressions of this view, while often strongly held, tended to be based on a simplistic translation of research evidence and practice in the US rather than a more detailed assessment of the nature of social factors in Northern Ireland. In the US the key arguments for desegregation were centred round the idea of equality. In Northern Ireland, by contrast, the primary arguments for integration were social.

Since these early debates, three main alternatives have been offered to account for the impact of segregated schools in Northern Ireland. The 'cultural hypothesis' suggested that segregated schools enhanced community divisions by introducing pupils to differing, and potentially opposing, cultural environments. This view emphasised differences in the curriculum of the separate school systems (Magee, 1970). The 'social hypothesis' suggested that, regardless of what was taught in schools, segregated schooling initiated pupils into conflict by emphasising and validating group differences and hostilities, encouraging mutual ignorance and, perhaps more important, mutual suspicion. This view emphasised the impact of segregation *per se* (Murray, 1983; 1985a; 1985b). The third view was that the issue of separate schools was largely irrelevant as a factor explaining the conflict and that the more accurate explanation was that it was based on material inequalities and injustice in Northern Ireland.

Although there was evidence available to provide support for all three of these perspectives, there was no clear consensus on which offered the most complete account of the impact of separate schools. In the absence of such a consensus, educationalists pursued three broad intervention strategies to try and promote reconciliation and tolerance through schools. The first involved curricular initiatives within the existing schools system. This was the approach adopted by some of the earliest intervention programmes, including the Schools Community Relations Project (1970) and the Schools Cultural Studies Project (1974), and was encouraged by the Department of Education in 1982. In the following year the Education for Mutual Understanding (EMU) programme was initiated. This programme encouraged schools, on a voluntary basis, to introduce themes related to community relations into their curriculum (McKernan, 1982; O'Connor, 1980; Taylor, 1992; Smith and Robinson, 1992).

The second broad strategy also worked within the context of segregated schools and sought to encourage contact programmes between pupils in Protestant and Catholic schools. In the early years these contact programmes faced problems because of their *ad hoc* and often transient character (Darby et al., 1977; Dunn et al., 1984). In an attempt to overcome some of these problems, the Inter-School Links project was established in 1986. The project established a contact programme between a number of Protestant and Catholic schools in a medium-sized town in Northern Ireland. The aim was to do this in a way that both integrated the contact work into the normal day-to-day activity of the schools and made it independent of any specific individuals (Dunn and Smith, 1989; Smith and Dunn, 1990). Other work in this area included special joint holiday schemes for young Protestants and Catholics.

The third strategy sought to develop integrated schools to serve both Protestant and Catholic pupils. An Act of Parliament in 1978 provided a basis for existing Protestant schools under state management to change status to integrated schools. In part because of the failure of schools to follow this option, a group of parents opened Lagan College in 1981, the first planned integrated school in Northern Ireland. Following the success of Lagan College other groups of parents came together to open planned integrated schools with the medium-term goal of having at least one primary and post-primary school in each of Northern Ireland's twenty-six District Council areas. These new schools are referred to as planned integrated schools as they consciously attempt to maintain a religious balance among their pupil enrolments and teacher workforce, and seek to reflect both cultural traditions in their curriculum (Moffat, 1993).

There was a great deal of overlap between these strategies. In particular there were close links between work on EMU and the contact schemes. It was clear too that official support for some of these initiatives was strengthened in the following ways: guidance material on EMU was produced and circulated to schools; the Cross Community Contact Scheme was initiated by the DENI in 1987 to provide funds for schools that wished to engage in contact programmes; some of the education and library boards appointed EMU Field Officers to support the work of teachers; and a variety of new agencies were opened, funded by government and charitable trusts, to provide support and advice to teachers.

The community relations dimension to education was strengthened still further by the Education Reform Order (ERO) (1989), the Northern Ireland version of the 1988 Education Reform Act (ERA) for England and Wales. In broad terms the ERO was closely modelled on the provisions of the ERA in that it introduced a statutory common curriculum for all schools, devolved greater managerial and financial powers to schools, and accorded a higher degree of school choice to parents. However, in contrast to the situation in England and Wales, where the issues of racial equality and multiculturalism appeared to be little more than an afterthought in the statutory curriculum, the Northern Ireland reform measures were more significantly influenced by community relations concerns. For the first time government took on the formal responsibility of supporting new initiatives towards the development of planned integrated schools. The main consequence of this was that the Department funded the Northern Ireland Council for Integrated Education in order to provide support and advice for parents wishing to establish new integrated schools. In addition, the ERO established a procedure whereby the parents of pupils in existing Protestant or Catholic schools could vote to transform the school to integrated status.

Alongside these measures on integrated schools, and in recognition of the likelihood that most pupils would continue to be educated in *de facto* segregated schools, the ERO required that EMU and Cultural Heritage would become compulsory cross-curricular themes in the Northern Ireland common curriculum. In other words, all schools in Northern Ireland would be required to reflect community relations themes in their curriculum. Under the themes of EMU and Cultural Heritage, schools would be encouraged, but not required, to engage in contact programmes. In other words, the measures contained in the ERO did not opt for any one of the strategies that had been developed within education over the previous years, but attempted to provide support for all the main strategic approaches.

Evaluating government initiatives

So what has been the impact of these measures? In the 1990s education formed a key part of the government's community relations strategy, with the expenditure on education forming a third of the entire community relations budget. Furthermore, within the education budget, a third was spent on contact programmes for pupils in Protestant and Catholic schools. A further quarter was spent in grant-aid to reconciliation bodies, many of which provided curriculum support for schools and a similar amount was spent on cultural traditions programmes.

Some consequences of this legislative and financial support are clear. The rate of increase in the opening of new integrated schools increased following the 1989 Education Reform Order and, over time, the proportion of post-primary schools has steadily increased. The money available to reconciliation bodies and through the contact programmes has led to the growth of a host of organisations which provide support for EMU work in schools, including statutory and voluntary organisations which offer training, materials, including videos, games, books, pamphlets and worksheets, on EMU-related themes. As a result of this, over time, a considerable body of expertise has developed from which teachers and schools can draw. It would be true to say that some of these resources and support would have been available even without an overarching government policy on community relations initiatives in schools. It is equally true to say, however, that the sheer amount of support available has been enhanced by the policy climate and the underpinning support of public money.

However, there remain some difficulties regarding the quality of the activity and its direct impact on community relations objectives. Three main reports have provided a picture of the work in schools: Smith and Robinson (1992) suggested that the EMU work lacked clear definition, thus leaving open the danger that the 'cutting edge' of the initiative could be lost if people focused on its less controversial and 'safe' aspects. There is reason to suppose this might occur: we have noted above that a 'social grammar' exists in Northern Ireland such that people tend to avoid talking about the issues of religion and politics in (religiously) mixed company (Gallagher, 1994). While broaching these issues can be considered 'impolite', this unwritten social rule means that people can engage in cross-community contact while remaining largely ignorant of the views of members of the 'other' community on the fundamental social divisions that exist within the society.

Smith and Robinson (1992) went on to suggest that there was a lack of coordination between the various statutory bodies with a responsibility for EMU, concerns about an over-emphasis on contact, as opposed to curricular, work within EMU, and that schools tended to accord the policy a relatively low priority. That EMU was seen by many as synonymous with 'contact' was further reinforced by classroom-based research in schools (Leitch and Kilpatrick, 1999) and, for many teachers, will have been reinforced by the financial priority given to contact, as seen above.

The difficulty with this over-emphasis on contact work is that a significant proportion of these programmes appeared to have limited value and, all too often, failed to address issues of division and conflict. In the worst cases they merely reproduced the degree of 'polite' contact that existed in the wider society which, as has been suggested above, is suffused with a social grammar of avoidance. More generally, an emphasis on contact programmes could limit the extent to which holistic work on community relations issues were addressed within schools if it encouraged a perception that community relations was the responsibility of only those limited numbers of teachers involved in contact programmes. And, despite the resources available, the numbers involved were quite small: Smith and Robinson (1996) estimated that while two-fifths of primary schools and three-fifths of post-primary schools were involved in contact work, this comprised only about a fifth and a tenth of pupils respectively. More recent data from the Department of Education suggests that in 2000/01 21 per cent of primary school pupils, but only three per cent of post-primary pupils were involved in funded contact programmes (O'Connor et al., 2002). They went on to argue that a refocusing of EMU work was needed to emphasise its whole-school dimensions, to highlight the implications for teaching and learning, to encourage teachers to address more controversial issues and to reduce the focus on contact work.

O'Connor et al. (2002) provided a detailed evaluation of the Schools Community Relations programme and identified some strengths in the work, including the commitment of education and library board officers and NGOs, and the undoubted commitment of some teachers who worked in this area. In addition, they identified the strength of long-term link programmes and the fact that there were examples of good practice. However, they also found that this work was often accorded a low strategic priority, that it lacked a coherent definition of community relations and strategy for evaluation, and that some school-links programmes lacked purpose. The study had been established to offer recommendations on future practice. O'Connor et al.'s recommendations covered a wide variety of issues, but at their heart were the ideas of extending funding support beyond simply contact work and encouraging a clearer examination of the purpose and strategic direction of any initiative. The recommendations in the report are currently out for consultation, but it seems likely that there will be some significant changes in this area in the future.

Research on the integrated schools has focused on a number of different aspects. Morgan et al. (1992a; 1992b), Agnew et al. (1992) and McEwen and Salters (1993) found that parents had a variety of motivations in sending their children to integrated schools, and sometimes they were preferred as a better alternative to secondary schools if a place could not be achieved in a grammar school. Despite this, claims that the integrated schools have a largely middle-class intake are unfounded: in 1998/99, for example, the median level of student entitled to free school meals in secondary schools was 41 per cent in Catholic schools, 26 per cent in Protestant schools and 25 per cent in integrated schools. A study into pupils in Lagan College, the longest established integrated school, found that friendship networks did cut across religious boundaries, so the school did seem to be providing a genuinely integrated environment (Irwin, 1993), a pattern confirmed in a later study in another school (McMullan, 2003). Gallagher et al. (1995) found that the second oldest integrated school (Hazelwood College) had developed innovative approaches to the curriculum and teaching, and staff were using the opportunity provided by an integrated setting to address issues related to social division and conflict. In addition, there is clear evidence that many within the integrated schools movement were innovative in the development of new curriculums and pedagogies to address issues related to a divided and conflicted society.

However, some research suggests that this aspect of the schools is being constrained, in part due to the turnover of staff and the limited specific training that is available for teachers wishing to work in integrated settings (Johnston, 2001). Other pressure arises from the enhanced accountability systems, the pressure of benchmarking and other performance-driven initiatives that draw time and energy from other activities, while other research suggests that the integrated schools sector may be characterised by weak systemic links and a consequent limited consistency in their internal organisation and practice (Milliken and Gallagher, 1998). The emergent problems are being addressed by the integrated schools movement, but they serve as a reminder that simply changing the structure of the schools does not, in itself, solve all the problems of a divided society – a more pro-active approach is not only needed, but arguably the problems of a divided society will only be addressed if they are constantly and explicitly being addressed.

Perhaps the biggest issue facing the integrated sector at present lies in the prospects for growth. Despite consistent majorities in social surveys saying that they would prefer integrated schools, currently only a little over four per cent of the total pupil population are in integrated schools (Gallagher et al., 2003). Most of the existing schools opened as entirely new schools following initiatives pursued by groups of parents. The government's preferred route of expansion is through the transformation of existing schools as a consequence of parental ballots because it is a more cost-effective route to change. In addition, there is already a surplus of places in schools and a significant demo-graphic downturn over the next decade. However, this raises a number of problems.

The first is that a transformation school has not just to develop a new ethos and character as an integrated school, but it has to do so by casting off an existing ethos and character. Existing evidence (McGonigle et al., 2003) suggests that while the transformation route can be difficult, and it is not always clear that everyone in a transform-ing school is fully involved in the process, in most cases the main par-ticipants do see it as a genuine process of change, as opposed to a more cynical manoeuvre, merely to keep a school open, for example. In order to ensure that any process of transformation represents a genuine process of change, the legislation governing the process requires that a school has a minimum 10 per cent minority enrolment at the point of transformation, and achieves a minimum minority enrolment of no less than 30 per cent within ten years. At the moment, however, only a very small number of schools (perhaps 40 in all), not all of which have shown any interest in the transformation option, meet this initial hurdle.

In addition, an attempt at transformation may produce negative consequences if not handled carefully. Within recent years, ballot decisions against transformation at a number of Protestant schools are reported to have led to a significant reduction in the number of Catholic applicants to both schools, although this is unconfirmed and may not be sustained. A further issue is that all of the transformed schools began life as Protestant, or controlled, schools. There is the potential for this to create a political problem if a perception grows within the Protestant community that it is 'their' schools that are being 'taken over' through this process of change. It is possible that there is a 'tipping-point' such that once the proportion of pupils at integrated schools reaches a certain, albeit low, level, then the entire system will rapidly tip-over towards integration, but it is not clear what, if any, conditions would be required for this tipping-point effect to occur. In the absence of such an effect then it seems likely that the growth of integrated schools will continue to be incremental, but slow, unless new models for integration develop. Two possibilities currently on the horizon are the possibility of jointly-run church schools, in line with joint Catholic/Anglican schools that operate in a number of English-speaking countries, or wider collaborative arrangements between schools, as was proposed following a review of post-primary provision in Northern Ireland (Burns, 2001).

Education and equality

Thus far we have concentrated on what might be described as the specifically educational aspects of community relations policy. However, the third leg of the government's approach to promoting better community relations in Northern Ireland has been a commitment to equality of opportunity. While the most obvious manifestation of this element of the policy was through legislation designed to outlaw discrimination on the basis of religion or political opinion, and an attempt to mainstream equity principles into the day-to-day work of government departments and other public bodies, there was an important educational dimension to this issue as well (Cormack and Osborne, 1983, 1991; Darby, 1991, 1997; Osborne and Cormack, 1987; Osborne et al., 1989; Edwards, 1995). As we have indicated above, in Northern Ireland the funding arrangements for Catholic schools followed practice in England. Thus, Catholic schools received public funds to cover a proportion of their capital costs. The difference represented the cost to the Catholic community of their right to own and operate their own school system. This type of arrangement is common in Europe and the principle was, in fact, confirmed in a case before the European Court of Human Rights when it was ruled that if a particular interest, such as a denominational authority, wanted to run its own schools then it should meet reasonable viability criteria before it is entitled to some public funds. The Court also ruled that it was reasonable to ask that particular interest to contribute towards the cost of the school in recognition of its ownership and control, or in other words, that it was not unreasonable for governments to provide less then 100 per cent funding.

In Northern Ireland two extra elements were added to the equation. First, there was a persistent pattern that leavers from Catholic schools had, on average, lower qualifications in comparison with leavers from Protestant schools. Second, there were labour market differences between Protestants and Catholics, to the disadvantage of Catholics, and the government was committed to the principle of fair employment. While discrimination contributed to the pattern of labour market difference, an investigation by the Standing Advisory Commission on Human Rights (SACHR) in the 1980s suggested that the differential performance of the two schools systems was also a contributory factor. As a result of this conclusion SACHR initiated research to investigate some of the reasons for this differential in attainment levels. The research suggested, among other things, that the different funding arrangements for Catholic schools had operated to their disadvantage and had probably contributed to the attainment difference. In an abstract sense it was reasonable to ask the Catholic community to make a financial contribution for their schools. However, on the basis of the wider context of government objectives, particularly the priority attached to fair employment, SACHR concluded that Catholic schools should be funded at the same levels as Protestant schools. After some public discussion on this issue the government agreed to this recommendation (Gallagher et al., 1994; for an update on these issues see Gallagher, 2003).

On one level this example could be seen as a positive example of a mature pluralism. If we accept the right of minority communities to organise their own school systems – which, as we will suggest below, seems to be consistent with international human rights standards – and to receive public funds for this, the decision to fund Catholic schools in Northern Ireland to the same level as state schools provided a demonstration of the government's commitment to equality. However, the decision and the research were criticised on a number of grounds. One of the criticisms was that the decision helped further to entrench segregated schools. Some critics suggested that it should have recommended developments in religiously integrated schools, although it remains a moot point whether a recommendation by SACHR for more integrated schools would have led to any additional increase in these schools. In any case the standards of the international community recognise and endorse the right of minorities to their own schools and, in so doing, differentiate between separate schools by choice and segregated schools by requirement (Caportorti, 1991; Churchill, 1996; Coulby, 1997; Craft, 1996).

But the main interest here is somewhat different. Now that all schools in Northern Ireland are entitled to full funding, has this led to an increase in cooperation between the school systems? This cooperation could include attempts to ensure that the separate schools do not unintentionally promote societal division. It could include pro-active attempts to promote tolerance, reconciliation and fairness through the schools. In addition, the authorities of the school systems could recognise that allowing for separate schools introduces an additional cost to the system as a whole and agree to collaborative initiatives designed to make the school systems more efficient. One way in which this might occur is for the transfer of property between the sectors in appropriate circumstances. This practical cooperation would avoid the bizarre situation that sometimes occurs where a school of one type closes as a school of another type is built from new on a nearby site.

In practice there is a level of cooperation between the school authorities, but arguably the opportunity for creative initiatives has not been
seized. And we have seen the situation where zero-sum arguments are
used by the authorities of Protestant and Catholic schools against the
development of religiously integrated schools. In other words, the
equity dimension in schools in Northern Ireland illustrates some of
the possibilities of pluralism, but it also illustrates the limitations, in
that in this case there are few examples in which a level playing-field
for funding has been used to identify opportunities for further development. Rather, in practice sectional interests are often prioritised. In
the examples outlined above we can see elements of a dilemma.
Changes were made to a situation in pursuit of the goal of equality, but
it could be argued that this change did not necessarily lead to greater
tolerance and reconciliation. Indeed some might argue that the main
result was to reinforce separation.

Education and the peace process

The peace process provides the most significant backdrop to current
educational developments. This process began in the early 1990s with
secret, and later open, negotiations between Republican paramilitaries
and the British and Irish governments, leading eventually to ceasefires
in 1994. For a variety of political reasons, significant progress was
delayed until after the 1997 elections in Britain and Ireland, but
progress then did lead to the establishment of working, if fragile, political institutions in Northern Ireland. These institutions seemed almost
always to be on the verge of collapse, but, at moments of crisis the
politicians managed to find some way to maintain progress. This was
so until October 2002 when the Assembly went into suspension.
Elections that had been planned for May 2003 were cancelled and
while it seemed likely that elections would be held in Autumn 2003,
there was little optimism that there would be a sufficient consensus to
get the Assembly up and running again.

Thus, the most significant feature of Northern Ireland in the early
years of the twenty-first century was not the achievement of peace, but
the fragility of the post-conflict institutions. The procedures in the
Assembly had been designed to promote coalition-building among the
political parties and thereby to develop trust: there was little evidence
that this had happened. Rather the fault-lines of politics seemed, as
ever, to revolve around religious and national identity. There had been
some hope that education might serve as a superordinate goal, on the

basis that most educational goals should stand above narrow sectional interests. In fact, educational debates have tended to be mediated through sectional lens: debates over resources have tended to revolve around allocations to the separate sectors, and claims and counter-claims on the fairness or otherwise of these decisions; pluralism in education has usually been addressed as the defence of separate institutional interests, with much less attention being given to innovative ways in which separate schools might reach across the institutional barriers in which they are embroiled; and even the recent debate over the future of academically selective schools at the post-primary level has seen a political split along largely Unionist and Nationalist lines (the former opposing change, the latter favouring change), even though the evidence suggests that selection has the greatest consequence for young people from different social backgrounds (Gallagher and Smith, 2001).

10
Dealing with Difference in Education

In 1929 Erich Maria Remarque published 'All Quiet on the Western Front' which went on to become one of the most influential pieces of fiction to appear in the interwar period. The book is based on Remarque's personal experience of trench warfare in World War One and, in chronicling the cruelty, horror and uselessness of war, provided a generation with the clearest expression of an anti-militaristic and anti-war message. The teacher, Kantorek, makes his first appearance in the novel when he cajoles and lectures his class of pupils until they all volunteer for active service. Following the jolt the young recruits receive when they actually experience the front-line, the central character of the book muses:

> Naturally we couldn't blame Kantorek for this. ... There were thousands of Kantoreks, all of whom were convinced that they were acting for the best – in a way that cost them nothing.

Just as the figure of Kantorek reminds us of the negative potential of education, so too the treatment meted out to the novel by the Nazis reminds us of the challenge ideas can provide to intolerance and hate. 'All Quiet on the Western Front' was one of numerous books banned by the Nazi state in Germany precisely because of its anti-militaristic message. At one point in the novel the teacher Kantorek refers to his class of young men as the 'Iron Youth', a term also used by Hitler when he declared in Mein Kampf that 'through sport and gymnastics ... boys should be hardened like iron'.

This was no fictional sentiment, of course, but one tiny element of a racial-ideological message that was to lead to the greatest crime of this century, and perhaps the greatest crime of any century. Nazi policy towards young people formed a crucial part of the overall strategy of the state. As in its attempts to remove all elements of an active and independent civil society within Germany, the Nazis dissolved or merged youth organisations outside their direct control into the Hitler Youth. Within three years of coming to power this objective had been achieved and an entire generation of German youth was taken through a coordinated series of interlinked organizations, including entry to the Jungvolk or Jungmadel for 10 year olds; progression to the Hitler Youth or League of German Maidens at age 14 years; and labour service for both sexes from age 18 years and membership, deemed voluntary, of one of the sections of the Nazi party.

In its education policy the Nazis pursued a variety of experimental models to create an ideologically secure leadership for the thousand-year Reich. National Political Educational Institutions (Napolas) were established as boarding schools on the sites of former Prussian military cadet schools. The Napolas were intended to train the functionaries of the Third Reich. They faced competition from the Adolf Hitler Schools (AHS) established by a different branch of the regime with the avowed purpose of training 'the Fuhrers of the future'. At the tertiary level a system of special colleges called the Ordensburgen was established. These emphasised military and sporting skills, allied with training in 'history' and 'racial science', and were loosely based on the perceived image and practice of the castles of the Teutonic knights. In numerical terms, none of these initiatives were of any great consequence: for example, there were less than two dozen Napolas or AHSs by the outbreak of the War. In part this was due to the chaotic nature of the Nazi state, where different branches worked in competition for Hitler's favour, notwithstanding the popular myth of German efficiency.

The curriculum of mainstream schools was influenced by chauvinist and racist values. The teaching of history in the schools was already infused with a heavily nationalist and anti-democratic orientation and so required little change. But the time and importance attached to sport was increased, and from September 1933, compulsory lessons in racial science were introduced, despite the virtual absence of textbooks and the fact that much of what was supposed to be taught was self-evidently contradictory. Some teachers nevertheless took it upon themselves to make extracts from the work of Hans Gunther available to pupils, or to introduce cranial measurement into lessons.

But the chaotic and contradictory nature of the message should not lead to the conclusion that the education policy of the Nazi state had no effect. In mainstream schools racial policy was actively and assiduously pursued, and its effects on minorities, particularly Jews and Roma, were, ultimately, murderous. In 1933 most Jewish teachers were dismissed from their posts. The few who were exempted due to their service on the front-line during the First World War were dismissed by 1935. Also in 1933 strict quotas were enforced on the proportion of children of 'non-Aryan' origin who were permitted to attend schools. After Kristellnacht, in 1938, Jewish children were excluded from German schools altogether, and by 1942 the remaining Jewish schools were closed down. By the late 1930s the Jewish children who still attended 'German' schools were often insulted publicly by teachers and pupils, made to sit at separate desks and forbidden from playing with 'Aryan' children during breaktimes.

In the first chapter we noted the debate between 'intentionalists' and 'fuctionalists' and the relative weight they placed on the aggressively anti-Semitic rhetoric of Hitler in the early years of the Nazi party. Whatever the merits of these arguments, there is clearly a connection between the discrimination actively expressed towards Jewish pupils by teachers and the pupils' peers in German schools, the identification and exclusion of Jews from public life in Germany and the occupied countries, and the transportation and mass murder of Jews in the camps in eastern Europe. The mass aspects of the racist ideology, in the spreading of which so many teachers and academics were eager and willing accomplices, helped to provide the 'ideational' climate within which mass murder could occur. It was this climate that led to the situation so aptly described by Allen (1989) in his study of a single German town during the Nazi state: most of the townsfolk did not actively discriminate against the town's few Jewish families, but when those families disappeared almost no one asked why, or where to? Another historian, Ian Kershaw (1984), made essentially the same point in his study of public opinion in Bavaria during the Nazi period when he said that the road to Auschwitz was built on hate, but paved with indifference.

After the war the mass murder carried out by the Nazi regime was condemned by the world, and the leaders of the regime that could be caught were tried and punished. The international community, through the UN, vowed that this should never happen again and declared genocide to be an international crime. But of course, mass killing as an instrument of political policy did happen again, in Cambodia, Rwanda, and, as noted also in the first chapter, in the succession wars of Yugoslavia. The ground-work for the last of these cases can be traced to nationalist ideologues in the Serbian Academy of

Sciences and Arts (Sibler and Little, 1996). In the 1980s, and under conditions of strict secrecy, the academicians drafted a memorandum which laid out a vision of how Yugoslavia should be in the future. Essentially it comprised a litany of Serbian nationalist grievances, claiming that the Serbs had suffered most in winning the Second World War, but gained the least. Their Serbian compatriots in Croatia, Bosnia and, especially, Kosovo, were described as being in an even more parlous state. It is not clear that the Academy intended to publish the memorandum, but extracts were published in newspapers in 1986, and it caused a convulsion within Yugoslavia. Practically all of the Communist leadership of the Federal state, and the federated republics, condemned the Academy and its nationalist agenda. All but one, for Slobodon Milosevic, leader of the Serbian Communist Party, atypically, remained silent on the memorandum and the Academy. Within the year Milosevic was to choose to play the Serbian nationalist card in Kosovo in order to secure his predominance in Serbia. He went on to use this nationalist agenda to cancel the autonomy of two regions within Serbia, before moving on to mobilise ethnic Serbs in Croatia and later Bosnia. That the collapse in Yugoslavia came so quickly and so bloodily should serve as a warning on the fragility of civilised society. We should give particular pause for thought given that the initial spark was put in place by academics. The mass killings of Bosnian Muslims is a reminder too of an observation by Kuper (1989) when he examined numerous historical examples of genocides and concluded that the most common characteristic of these events was that the perpetrators and victims were of different religious communities.

Traditionally, of course, we have tended to think of the role of mass education systems in maintaining stability and reinforcing unity within state territories. Historically, and in more recent times, we can see examples of how the education systems of states played a key role in maintaining this fictive image of the culturally homogeneous nation-state. Coulby (1997) has highlighted some of the social processes through which education sought to make real this condition, including the naturalisation of citizens towards a defined common base, the invention of a canon of 'national' literature, the use, in Europe, of a particular version of neo-classicism to 'explain' the progressive evolution of European civilisation from Ancient Greece to the present, and the promulgation of a common national language. In all these process, Coulby suggests, schools and universities played a significant and influential role. Churchill (1996) goes further to suggest that the traditional notion of the nation-state embodied a set of assumptions which simultaneously claimed, and tried to construct, linguistic, cultural and political homogeneity. Public schooling contributed to this process by imparting a common culture, through an official language, that involved a common accepted set of behaviours, including civic loyalty.

It is straightforward to identify historical examples of these processes. The development of mass education systems towards the end of the nineteenth century played a role in unifying nations at a time when the democratic franchise was being extended. This was as true of 'old' societies, such as Britain, where the schools could promulgate tradition and history, or 'new societies', such as the US where schools acted as part of the 'melting-pot' fusing a multitude of migrant communities into American citizens. Towards a somewhat different purpose, but following essentially similar processes, the nascent USSR education system served as a mechanism for constructing 'Soviet man' (Bowen, 1981). This role for education is not only historical.

The Central Asian Republics of the former USSR provide an example of the process of nation-building in two distinct circumstances (Akiner, 1997), the invention and reinvention of the state through education. When these territories came under Soviet control they were delineated into separate Republics. Building a sense of nationhood in each area took longer, but included a range of strategies. Some of the numerically larger communities were accorded privileges, such as access to key positions in society and politics, other communities were accorded certain rights, including educational and linguistic rights, while smaller communities were, at various times, subsumed within larger groups or reclassified out of existence. Other aspects of the creation of national identities included the creation of national languages and the compilation of 'national' histories that were selective and presented within the wider Soviet framework. In particular, while the Republic was described as providing the 'national' identity, the Soviet Union provided the identity of 'citizenship'. There was a more explicitly coercive aspect to the process also, with particular social dimensions targeted for removal, including Islam. After 1991 these Republics gained independence when the USSR imploded, and renewed efforts at nation-building, this time to specifically distance the nations from the Soviet experience, began. In this second wave of nation-building there is a resurgence of national culture, rewriting of the 'national' histories, a resurgence of Islam and schools now teach the Arabic script. All these initiatives occur in a situation where the new histories are deliberately contestatory, in that they set out to challenge the hitherto assumed European/Russian superiority, the ritual of the nation is being rapidly reinvented, or simply invented for the first time, and a pre-Soviet basis for the rights of occupation and control are being established. None of this is to deny the legitimacy of the newly independent states, but rather to use them as illustrative of the processes that all states go through. Furthermore, many of the processes can be addressed through the education system and many are addressed most efficiently in this way.

Another example can be seen in Namibia. Nahas Angula, who was to become the first Minister of Education in independent Namibia, wrote, in 1986, that schools should 'aim at fostering patriotic culture, national unity, respect and appreciation of the Namibian culture, love for work, personal integrity, pan-Africanism and a progressive outlook towards humanity' (cited in Norkvelle, 1995: p. 363). Namibia had been under the illegal occupation of South Africa from 1915 to 1990 at which point independence and democracy were achieved. Education policy prior to independence had mirrored the apartheid education system with ethnic and racial separation allied with highly unequal provision for the different groups. At independence there was a move to establish English as the language of instruction in schools, despite the fact that Afrikaans was more widely spoken, was the common language in most education regions of the country, and was the language in which most schoolbooks were published. More generally, a new curriculum was introduced with great speed: the curriculum itself was finalised in six weeks. While there were a variety of factors which influenced the scope and speed of these changes after independence, in a manner contrary to the government's commitment otherwise to consultation, Jansen (1995) suggests that the main reason for this approach was to demonstrate a change from the apartheid *status quo* as quickly as possible. There were, Jansen suggested, few ways in which the new government could materially signal a fundamental step away from the old regime, but education policy provided one way.

But the nation-building role of education does raise the question of whether or not the discourse of citizenship speaks equally to all people living within the state. The harsh reality, of course, is that this is not so, especially when, as in its traditional role, education has been used as an instrument for assimilation. Such an approach relies on two assumptions, first, that there is a common unitary culture or identity within mainstream society and, second, that the burden of responsibility for any change lies with any new arrivals into that homogeneous context. In fact, of course, societies are heterogeneous and this is now generally recognised, even where the perceived demands of nation-building lead to the privileging of a unitary national identity over the particularistic identities to be found within society. Even in these situations, however, the legitimisation of difference raises a new set of policy options, particularly in education. Throughout this book most of the case study examples that have been examined have adopted differing structural responses to societal pluralism. One approach, as in the US and Britain, is to establish a system of common schools within which the pluralism within society will be reflected. The main alternative is to allow minorities to run their own school systems, and thereby to provide a plurality of institutions, rather than plural institutions *per se*. This last objective can be approached either through parallel school systems for majority and minority communities, as in Northern Ireland or, in the past, in apartheid South Africa, or through distinctive schools or curriculums in different parts of a state, as in the federal states of Europe.

The main emergent theme from the examination of the case studies in this book is that no specific structural arrangement provides a guaranteed outcome: there is as much variation within the categories of cases as there is between them. To the extent that any particular approach has been successful, this has occurred within distinctive historical and social contexts. This does not mean we operate in a social vacuum: the international community, through the UN, has established agreed trans-national frameworks for the rights and responsibilities of peoples to one another, and the policy and practice of states towards their societies (Caportorti, 1991). Within these internationally agreed frameworks it is possible to identify the broad principles within which educational policy and practice should develop (Minority Rights Group, 1994), and it is these principles that should be our guide towards a world where education systems contribute towards the realisation of human potential in a context of fairness and social inclusion. Central to this guide is the principle of equality and it is this to which we now turn as one of the key features of struggles for democratic education over the past century has been to roll back inequalities in educational practice.

My starting-point is provided by some of the main themes to emerge from a recent book on equality in education by Kenneth Howe (Howe, 1997). His discussion is centred around three main themes. I will briefly describe them and then consider each in a little more detail. The first theme is a challenge to the received wisdom that a basic understanding of equality has to differentiate, and choose between equality of opportunity and equality of results. The second is a consideration of a just basis for a distributive approach by the state. And the third is a consideration of what he describes as the core principles underpinning an approach to equality. The remainder of the book involves an application of his philosophical conclusions in a number of specific policy contexts.

Howe's first theme is to challenge the idea that equality of opportunity is conceptually distinct from equality of results. A formalist position argues that equal opportunity can only be understood in terms of the provision of opportunity. If people choose not to avail of the opportunity and unequal outcomes obtain, then that is entirely a matter for the individuals concerned. By contrast, an actualist position argues that it is only possible to know that equal opportunity is provided if equal outcomes emerge. In this view equality can only be judged in terms of outcomes. Howe challenges this dichotomy by differentiating between meaningful opportunities and bare opportunities. Not all opportunities are equally meaningful or worth wanting, and in order for an opportunity to be meaningful it is necessary that it fulfills a number of conditions. First, people must know that the opportunity is available. Second, they should be provided with sufficient information in order that they can make a reasoned choice about its value. Third, they should be aware of the consequences of taking or not taking the opportunity. And finally, they should already have a level of skills or knowledge that will allow them to use and gain from the opportunity. This last criterion is important. There would be little point, for example, in simply admitting some people to higher education as part of an access strategy unless they had already achieved a minimal level of education or were provided with special support. Otherwise the opportunity provided to them would be of little enduring value.

Thus, what Howe is saying is that meaningful opportunities are ones that provide a genuine option for individuals, whereas bare opportunities are ones that exist only in some theoretical or literal sense, but not in any practical sense. He then goes on to suggest that an educational opportunity at any point takes on a tree-like character in that the range of meaningful opportunities that is available crucially depends on the experience and knowledge they have gained up to that point. Depending on the results they have already achieved, only some branches of the tree that stretch out ahead of them are available in any meaningful way. In making this point Howe has turned the conventional debate between formalist and actualist positions on its head. It is no longer the case, he argues, that we need to differentiate between equality of opportunity and equality of results, since the provision of meaningful opportunity only makes sense in the context of prior results. The key issue in delivering equality, in other words, is now refocused almost completely on results. Thus, the issues that drive policy should be to ask: what kind of educational results do we need to equalise in order to provide meaningful opportunities? And to what extent should these results be equalised?

The second element in Howe's argument follows from this and concerns the just basis for a distributive approach to equality policy. He begins by examining three frameworks that arise from the liberal political tradition: the libertarian, utilitarian and liberal-egalitarian positions. Libertarians oppose a redistributive approach by government on grounds of principle, since they privilege the principle of individual liberty and place strict limits on state action. For radical libertarians the law should require parents to educate their children, but the state would only pay for the education of the very poorest, and would require only a mere handful of civil servants to run this minimalist service. However, since the libertarian position provides no basis for meaningful opportunity it seems clear that it provides no principled basis for equality.

Howe next considers the utilitarian argument. This view suggests that education should be evaluated in terms of its impact on economic activity. Educational intervention can be justified on the grounds that it maximises the collective economic benefit to society by dealing with the wasteful consequences of social disadvantage. Unlike a libertarian, the utilitarian has no problem with a distributive state. The problem, however, is that the principle of equality of opportunity has a fragile existence within the utilitarian framework.

This fragility is well illustrated in Brighouse's (2000) discussion of the role of equality in selective schooling systems. Many of the debates over the relative merits of selective and comprehensive school systems revolves around the impact of each system on the average performance of pupils. However, as Brighouse points out, this is an overly narrow criterion on which to judge the two systems as it seems to be based on a wholly utilitarian argument that the best outcome for the greatest number will emerge from a particular system, and therefore that system ought to be used. However, the answer really depends on the commitment to equality of opportunity, because a selective system could have a higher average performance level alongside a more unequal distribution of performance. In other words, it is conceivable to imagine a set of circumstances where the aggregate educational or economic outcomes are maximised by practices that are also characterised by a high level of inequality. If policy is driven primarily by utilitarian principles, in other words, there is no *a priori* reason to assume that equality of opportunity will have a high status.

Howe's favoured position is a liberal-egalitarian one. There are various specific approaches within this framework, but they all share a concern to limit the extent to which inequality operates within society. Thus, they agree, on principle, with a redistributive approach by the state, while also recognising the value of dynamic markets, the importance of economic exchange and the acceptability of some level of inequality within society. The liberal-egalitarian principle favoured by Howe is a threshold one. He sees a number of advantages in the idea of a threshold. First, the threshold is an individual good, as a certain level of education provides the basis for an individual to achieve other goods such as income, employment and health. Second, the threshold is a social good, because it contributes to other social goods and because a highly unequal society limits the ability of some citizens to exercise the rights of citizenship – such a society is a democracy in name only. Third, this approach is needs-based in that different individuals need varying levels of support to achieve the threshold – in this way it provides a legitimate basis for differential treatment. Finally, the approach is results-based and falls towards the interventionist end of strategies for equality, but it avoids the need for strict egalitarianism, as beyond the threshold individuals are free to pursue their own ends and choice plays an increasing role. Howe puts it this way: 'while the threshold limits the principles of both liberty and utility, it eliminates neither'(p. 27). Howe defines his notion of the education threshold as the 'participatory educational ideal'. He prefers this to the alternative notion of equality as compensation as invariably this involves little negotiation on whether opportunities are actually worth having. Compensatory approaches are criticised from the political right on the grounds that they sap individual initiative and constrain freedom of choice. But they are criticised also from the left on the grounds that they secure relations of domination and subordination by presenting particular definitions of educational worth as if they were universal.

Critical theory developed as neo-Marxists decamped from economic determinism to incorporate broader dimensions of identity, such as gender, race and ethnicity, and offered challenges to the taken-for-granted assumptions about worth that are embedded in so many social institutions, including schools. It is possible to reject the naïve utopianism of some of these accounts, or the self-indulgent narcissism of others, while at the same time recognising that, at their core, they have a point. The point, however, can be addressed by the participatory dimension to equal opportunity. In the remainder of his book Howe tests the value of his philosophical claims by applying them to a range of policy areas including gender equality, ability grouping, testing and parental choice. For present purposes the main interest lies in Howe's application of the participatory ideal to the issue of multiculturalism.

Multiculturalism is linked to the issue of group identity and, more particularly, the diverse identities that exist within any society. We can accept the postmodernist notion that identities are politically important, that they are contingent and that they are linked to patterns of advantage and disadvantage. However, although postmodernists rail against metanarratives, or grand explanations, education does not appear to make any sense unless it is for a purpose. Thus, alongside the critical element derived from postmodernism, educationalists can also accept the idea that different identities can only be accommodated if certain core democratic principles are shared across all groups. The dilemma this creates is that the common core has to be defined in some way, but it should not be so linked to one group that other diverse identities are negated. The solution is to find ways to recognise alternative identities and perspectives through the schools. Following Gutman (1987), Howe suggests that this can be achieved through the establishment of a democratic threshold which is the education that young people need in order to allow them to participate as equals in the democratic process. Gutman's notion of the democratic threshold includes the principles of tolerance and non-repression. Tolerance here is taken to mean the acknowledgement of difference, while non-repression means that education cannot be used to deny consideration of alternative perspectives.

For Howe both principles are too weak. It is possible to acknowledge difference, to listen to an alternative perspective, and then to ignore it. The danger, then, is that despite the principles of tolerance and non-repression, minorities may still be placed in the dilemma of having to choose between maintaining their group identity or enjoying full rights of democratic participation. In order to provide adequate protection for marginalised or excluded groups a higher standard is required. Howe suggests this can be provided by the participatory ideal. In place of the inadequate virtue of tolerance, Howe argues for the 'virtue of recognition' as this implies an acceptance not only that group identities are different, but also that they are equal. In place of the inadequate principle of non-repression, he offers the principle of non-oppression. While non-repression implies that alternative perspectives should be heard, the principle of non-oppression implies that certain marginalised or excluded perspectives should be provided with special protection to guarantee their place in the public domain in order to delegitimise assimilation.

Although he approaches the issue from a very different direction, Ramon Flecha arrives at a very similar conclusion in his consideration of the role education can play in combating racism (Flecha, 1999). Flecha's central claim is that there are two forms of racism. The older form is based on a claim of the superiority of one group over another, and it is this claim that anti-racists frequently attack. However, a more contemporary form of racism, based on postmodern relativism, accepts diversity and difference, but accords different groups a place in their own, distinctive contexts. By refusing to affirm the universal values of dialogue and interdependence, these postmodern versions of racism promote separation and exclusive ways of living. While allowing difference to exist, they assign different groups to their own distinctive social spaces.

Flecha (1999) offers an alternative possibility based on the principles of dialogue and interdependence, underpinned by an explicit commitment to equality. In his article he talks of interdependence in terms of hybridisation, the dynamic basis, he argues, for change and development. He argues that an orientation towards dialogue and hybridism are worthwhile goals as 'no culture in Europe can survive without communicating with other cultures, taking elements from them, and developing new cultural components from this exchange'. Further, he argues that those who seek to promote nostalgia for the 'original' culture or identity are, in fact, distorting history by failing to recognise, or accept, that present cultures and identities arose from a process of dialogue and hybridisation. This conservative nostalgia 'ultimately provokes racism and the rejection of dialogue with others by perceiving dialogue as a threat to the original culture's identity'.

Schools have a potentially crucial role to play in the process. The traditional role of education has been to promote a sense of national unity through assimilation, but for Flecha the promotion of dialogic processes within schools, involving not only teachers and students, but also parents and communities, will help to promote an orientation towards equality of differences. Following this Flecha goes on to suggest that we need an approach to diversity in education which is both pluricultural and intercultural. It needs to be pluricultural in order to allow all individuals and groups to live their differences, and it needs to be intercultural to allow them the opportunity to exchange and share new forms of living. This approach to dialogue, intercommunication and interdependence celebrates the participatory and inclusive possibilities of democracy, but sees the need to extend democratic practice in order to ensure that the promise remains fulfilled. Howe's articulation of a democratic threshold in education, based on the participatory ideal, offers one set of principles through which Flecha's vision might be realised.

Having discussed the participatory principle in equality, I now want to turn to the issue of the common school, traditionally the primary basis for social integration through assimilation (Coulby, 1997; Churchill, 1996). The positive claim of assimilation was to promote social unity and integration by constructing the imagined community of the nation. But the reality was that the discourse of citizenship did not speak equally to all members of society, leading to progressive struggles for recognition and inclusion. In Chapters 5 and 6 we examined the example provided by the US where there have been successive struggles against legal and informal segregation in schools, for affirmative action and for a multicultural curriculum. In Chapter 7 we examined the case of Britain where it is possible to trace a similar line of development from an assimilationist period, where the presence of minorities was seen to be the problem, through periods when multicultural and anti-racist initiatives have been promoted. In both examples – the USA and Britain – education has traditionally denied or downplayed difference, but in both cases acknowledgement of diversity in education became official policy.

In his 1994 book Maurice Berube traced the history of various reform movements in US education and highlighted the victory of the multicultural movement over, on one hand, the traditionalists who advocated assimilation, and, on the other hand, the Afrocentrists who advocated the racial separation of schools. Despite this, however, the last 20 years have seen a diminished legal basis for pro-active measures for equality and desegregation. In fact, the only time the Supreme Court adopted a pro-active approach was between the Brown decision in 1954 and the Milliken decision in 1974. A succession of Republican Presidents have altered the political balance of the Court and created an environment where schools are now resegregating (Orfield and Yun, 1999). This in turn is producing a crisis for the idea of the common school in the US. In many senses the same situation pertains in Britain. The high point of the multicultural and equality agenda in education should have followed the 1985 Swann Report. But while this commission was established under a Labour government, it reported under a Conservative one, and its call for a pluricultural curriculum for all schools was largely ignored as the marketisation processes of the Education Reform Act were rolled out. As we saw in Chapter 7, the Labour government elected in 1997 seemed more committed to economic priorities that social ones, and seemed to hope that its commitment to social justice would become more manifest once economic conditions had produced significant improvements generally.

Both examples called into question the ability of the common school to give voice to the diverse interests that existed within societies, and raised again the dichotomy that has informed debates on the role of education in divided societies for many years. Essentially this debate revolves around the alternative polarities of, on the one hand, common schools which seek to represent the diversity of society within one institution and, on the other hand, separate schools, which allow diverse interests to run their own schools as the best way to provide minorities with a mechanism for maintaining their identity. Clearly this is a debate which has been and remains highly relevant to the situation in Northern Ireland, as considered in Chapter 9.

In that example we saw that many external commentators, and not a few internal ones, suggested that the system of separate schools for Protestants and Catholics had contributed to community division, and that the establishment of integrated schools would contribute to social harmony. As we saw in Chapter 9, the education system in Northern Ireland was, and is, religiously segregated, with only a small proportion of students attending integrated schools. Many people think of this situation as akin to educational apartheid, as in pre-democratic South Africa (Chapter 8), or as analogous to the segregated schools in the Southern states of the US (Chapter 5). Both examples highlighted the negative potential of separate schools and were used to promote calls for the development of common schools for all pupils in Northern Ireland, even though this ignored the difference between separate systems where minorities opt out on the basis of choice and segregated systems where institutional restrictions are imposed on minorities.

It is possible to identify contexts where separate schools are part of a strategy for social harmony as in the Dutch system of pillarisation. There is, in fact, an interesting contrast between the Netherlands and Belgium. When they separated in the first half of the nineteenth century the Netherlands opted for a common language and religious diversity, while Belgium opted for a common religion and linguistic diversity. History would suggest that the Dutch version has been more successful in promoting social integration. This further underpins the central argument of this book that structural change in education does not guarantee predictable results. The traditional idea of the common school was rooted in assimilationist assumptions, but these were cast off in most places as societal diversity was acknowledged. However, the experience of many common school systems is that they have failed to realise the promise of diversity. In the same vein, we can identify education systems where institutional separation has been used to promote division, and others where separate systems are part of a strategy for an accommodation of diversity. But if particular educational structures will not guarantee progressive social results, then what, if anything, can we do to contribute to social harmony? I would now like to focus my discussion on some ideas that might help, ideas which connect with some of the ideas already discussed earlier. This new source is derived from a defence of the idea of the US common school as advocated by Walter Feinberg (1998).

Between the extremes of assimilation and separation, Feinberg identities two alternative positions, which he terms pluralism and multiculturalism, and for which he offers very particular definitions. Unlike assimilationists, pluralists do not urge schools to ignore or remain indifferent to cultural diversity. Pluralists agree that schools should teach pupils to respect individuals from different cultures, but they do not agree that schools should, as a matter of course, actively promote different cultural identities. The rationale for this is that the pluralist believes in the existence of a common core of values and principles which should be inculcated through schools in order to provide a basis for common interest and as a means of promoting social integration. Pluralists seek equality among individuals in the public sphere and freedom of association in the cultural sphere. The role of schools is to create the conditions under which choices exist, but not necessarily to promote all available options.

By contrast, multiculturalists, in Feinberg's understanding, reject the demarcation between the public and the cultural spheres. They argue that in the public sphere particular cultural interests are already embedded as if they were universal interests. By contrast, they want to establish the public sphere as a cornucopia of cultural options, a bazaar rather than a court. In education this requires a commitment to promote different identities as part of a strategy of inclusion, while also rejecting separatism in favour of cultural fairness, that is, the creation of spaces where no one culture dominates over others. Thus, in Feinberg's analysis, muilticulturalists offer the notion of cultural fairness as an alternative to the common core of values offered by the pluralists. Feinberg seeks to defend a version of pluralism, based on the notion of a common core of values, and begins by contending with two challenges that advocate different forms of separatism. The first challenge comes from communitarians who argue that common schools cannot provide a basis for an adequate morality, while the second is based on a culturalist or relativist view that suggests that the common school cannot provide a neutral context within which different identities will be fairly represented.

The first of these challenges argues that the common school is indifferent to particular moral codes and thereby weakens the link between one generation and the next. On this basis the communitarian seeks separate schools in order to ensure that appropriate moral norms are taught. Some who take this position go on to argue that the moral bases provided by the communally-based separate schools actually promotes wider cultural tolerance because they are so clearly rooted in specific cultural communities. In the US there are a number of versions of this argument, including those who argue that the academic success of Catholic schools is linked to their values base and the sense of social capital they develop within the strong communal context of the school (Bryk et al., 1993), or those who support charter schools in order to create networks of distinctive options for parents.

In Feinberg's view this challenge is based on a confusion of two separate claims. The first is that moral norms are communally grounded, which is unproblematic, while the second is that moral norms are communally bounded. For Feinberg the second claim is problematic, particularly in the context of a multicultural society. The main problem is that, in education, this claim sets the communal interest over that of the child while simultaneously ignoring the fact that, in a liberal society, the freedom to assert communal identity exists within a wider context of democratic rights and responsibilities. Once members of a cultural community acknowledge that they are part of a multicultural society, then the communal interest cannot form the only basis through which education contributes to the formation of self. This is so because the obligations that flow from communal membership now extend to include obligations that flow from societal membership. One of the responsibilities included within this is the responsibility of society to provide all children with certain options, so long as this is within a context where diversity is respected; essentially this is the liberal criterion of autonomy or choice.

The second challenge is based on quite different grounds. It argues, on relativist grounds, that all cultural identities are equally valid, and that their worth only make sense within their own contexts. Since common schools privilege one criteria of worth over others, they necessarily end up imposing one identity over others. Common schools cannot therefore provide a neutral basis for identity formation, but will end up damaging the identities of minorities. Feinberg opposes this claim on a number of grounds. A key basis of his critique focuses on the implicit notion that different cultural identities are incommensurate, that is that their different truth-systems provide no basis for intercultural communication. The reality is that culture and identity are dynamic entities involved in interdependent relationships with other cultural and identity formations. Feinberg also critiques the claim that common schools will necessarily damage minority identity. Part of the problem with this position is that it casts education as an inevitably negative force, or else freezes educational action permanently. Furthermore, it ignores the problem of neglect that can arise if walls are built between cultural communities. The critique of the problem of neglect claims that, not only is interdependence and intercultural communication the normal condition, but that we all benefit from it and are enriched by it.

Thus, Feinberg is able to claim that there are grounds to defend the idea of the common school against critics who would seek separate schools on either communitarian or culturalist grounds. Given that he has already rejected the assimilationist position that schools should consciously promote one identity, the question then lies in the extent to which common schools should provide space for many identities. Here he engages with the tension between his pluralist position and a multiculturalist position. His essential argument is that the difference between them is not as wide as it might seem. There are two main consequences of multicultural education. The first relates to the way members of one community will be informed and feel about others. The second relates to the way they will be informed and feel about their own community (p. 131). The traditionalist critics focus on the second of these, claiming that the pursuit of communal pride results in curriculum decisions that are made on political rather than educational grounds. Schlesinger (1991) offers a version of this argument when he criticizes the use of history as therapy. The alternative position is that the active promotion of a sense of self-worth is necessary in order to ameliorate the consequences of years of oppression. In the US much of the practical focus of this dispute has revolved around the appropriate canon of literature, although it played a key role in the debate over the history curriculum (Nash et al., 2000)

Feinberg tries to find another way. The history and life of a multicultural society is expressed through the many stories and scripts that make up the experience of different communities. Feinberg suggests that pluralists and multiculturalists agree that schools should present the right scripts, but differ on what those scripts ought to be. But for Feinberg no one script fully articulates the position of a community as 'the struggle between them is as much about future identities as it is about past experience' (p. 154). Feinberg then suggests a dynamic process where an understanding of change is as important as anything else:

> The error is to think that children must locate themselves exclusively within one or other of these scripts. Rather, multicultural thinking skills ultimately entail students coming to understand the various stories about cultural and national identity <u>as scripts</u> that are presented for them to validate, challenge, negotiate, and rewrite. (p. 154).

In a memorable phrase he suggests that the provision of many scripts has a comparative value in that they can be used: '... with one another as tools for reflection and understanding and not as the choreography of an old dance'. (p. 156)

The question then arises to which identities and scripts ought to be recognised within common schools. As we have already seen, Feinberg eschews any *a priori* commitment to acknowledge all identities, but he attempts to set conditions for recognition. All identities are entitled to minimal recognition as this is an important part of the liberal ideal of respecting each individual and teaching children about different conceptions of worth (p. 168). It entails an awareness by the teacher of the cultural background of different pupils and the implications this might have for classroom practice. The question lies in who should be entitled to robust recognition. Here Feinberg defines two criteria. Prior to these is a criterion of economic need, but this is an entitlement that relates to administrative rather than group categories. It does, however, link into his first criterion of standing, when robust recognition of group position is necessary in order to raise the standing of a hitherto marginalised or excluded group. But this is a group-based entitlement rather than a group right *per se*.

The second is a criterion based on historical injustice and the acknowledgement of the debt created by past violations of rights and liberties. Attending to these debts is an important part of the overall narrative of the community as a whole because of the challenge they pose to the taken-for-granted character of the dominant narratives:

> Here robust recognition involves shining the spotlight on these separate chapters, enabling those inside to hear them acknowledged by those outside and enabling those outside to hear them told by those inside. (p. 189)

For Feinberg then the role of the common school in a multicultural society is to provide a citizenship education that promotes respect for self and others, encourages the growth of cultural competence and develops towards cultural understanding. The value of the last of these is that the ability to see and hear alternative cultural frames from the inside reminds us not only of their contingent nature, but also of the contingent nature of our own cultural frame. The criteria for robust recognition provides particular identities with special claims to being placed directly within the common school. Their scripts and stories are to form a key part of the dialogue through which children from all traditions, but especially the dominant ones, come to understand their society better.

In some situations the establishment of common schools, however desirable, will take time and may, in any case, be confounded by other factors, including demographic realities. What is the relevance of these ideas to such circumstances and do they provide us with any insights into finding the basis for a more positive contribution by schools?

One of the emergent arguments of this book is that we will not guarantee that our schools will play their fullest role in promoting reconciliation in our society merely by changing educational structures. In some sense this may be analogous to the statistical fixation which avoids the tougher conversation over the nature of equality. In the equality agenda the empirical evidence is an aid to understanding, but is not an end. The discussion needs to be extended to articulate a wider vision of what the condition of equality entails and what needs to be done to achieve it. In Howe's terms we need to delineate the things that need to be equalised and the extent to which they should be equalised in order to produce meaningful opportunities. In addition, we need to consider additional and innovative ways in which participative and dialogic processes can be established to promote more inclusive decision-making and to clarify where equality sits on the order of priorities.

So, too, in education. The contention is that no structure for organising an education system provides guarantees on a harmonious future. Rather the key lies in the establishment of dialogic processes in and between inclusive institutions, providing for a range of possible futures. Rather than prescribing a particular future, rather seek to provide a set of inclusive institutions through which the journey might be made. A debate over future structures risks freezing action in the present. That said, in situations where separate schools exists, either by choice or by default, this only makes it even more necessary to establish the virtue of recognition in all the schools, with robust recognition of the voices and perspectives that have been traditionally marginalised or excluded. To paraphrase Feinberg, we need to shine the spotlight on those different scripts, enabling those inside to hear them acknowledged by those outside, and enabling those outside to hear them told by those inside. The key, I think, is to promote participative dialogue and to ensure that absent voices are made present, to develop, in schools, the interweave of interconnections which Varshney (2002) identified as being key to the maintenance of inter-ethnic harmony in India.

Towards the end of his book Walter Feinberg quotes William Galston when he says that the willingness to put forward your views intelligently and candidly in order to persuade rather than manipulate or coerce is a critical factor in a democratic society. Feinberg then goes on to remind us that this willingness is learned. For schools and teachers, therefore, the key task in enabling young people to become engaged and participating citizens is to develop among them 'an awareness of how everybody has a responsibility for creating a climate in which this willingness can arise'(p. 238).

References

Abzug, R.H. (1985) *Inside the vicious heart*, Oxford: Oxford University Press.

Adorno, T.W., Frenkel-Brunswik, E., Levinson, D.J., and Sanford, R.N. (1950) *The Authoritarian Personality*, New York: Harper.

Agnew, U., McEwen, A., Salters, J. and Salters, M. (1992) *Integrated Education: The Views of Parents*, School of Education, The Queen's University of Belfast.

Aguado, T. and Malik, B. (2001) 'Cultural diversity and school equality: intercultural education in Spain from a European perspective', *Intercultural Education*, 12(2), pp. 149–162.

Akbar, M.J. (1985) *India: The Seige Within*, England: Penguin Books.

Akenson, D.H. (1970) *The Irish Education Experiment: the national system of education in the nineteenth century*, London: Routledge and Kegan Paul.

Akenson, D.H. (1973) *Education and enmity: the control of schooling in Northern Ireland*, London: David and Charles.

Akiner, S. (1997) 'Melting pot, salad bowl – cauldron? Manipulation and mobilization of ethnic and religious identities in Central Asia', *Ethnic and Racial Studies*, London: Routledge, 20(2), pp. 362–398.

Allemann-Ghiondas, C. (1994) 'Switzerland and its educational system: from Babylon to Multiculturalism', *Zeitschrift fur Padagogik*, Germany: Beltz, 40(1), pp. 127–145.

Allen, W.S. (1989) *The Nazi Seizure of Power: the experience of a single German town 1922–1945*, Harmondsworth: Penguin.

Allport, G.W. (1954) *The Nature of Prejudice*, USA: Addison-Wesley.

Anderson, B. (1983) *Imagined communities: reflections on the origin and spread of nationalism*, London: Verso.

Arad, Y., Gutman, Y. and Margaliot, A. (eds) (1981) *Documents on the Holocaust: selected sources on the destruction of the Jews of Germany and Austria, Poland, and the Soviet Union*, Jerusalem/Oxford: Yad Vashem/Pergamon Press.

Ascher, C. (1993) 'The changing face of racial isolation and desegregation in urban schools', *ERIC/CUE Digest 91*, New York: ERIC Clearinghouse on Urban Education.

Audit Commission (1996) *Trading Places: the Supply and Allocation of School Places*, London: Audit Commission.

Bacal, A. (1991) 'Ethnicity in the Social Sciences', *CRER Reprint Paper in Ethnic Relations 3*, England: Centre for Research in Ethnic Relations.

Bach, D.C. (1989) 'Managing a plural society: the boomerang effects of Nigerian Federalism', *Journal of Commonwealth and Comparative Studies*, London: Frank Cass, 27(2), pp. 218–245.

Ball, S.J., Bowe, R. and Gewirtz, S. (1997) 'Circuit of schooling: a sociological exploration of parental choice of school in social-class contexts', in Halsey, A.H., Lauder, H., Brown, P. and Wells, A.S. (eds), *Education: culture, economy, society*, Oxford: Oxford University Press.

Ball, S.J., Bowe, R. and Gewirtz, S. (1994) 'Market forces and parental choice: self-interest and competitive advantage in education', in Tomlinson, S. (ed) *Educational Reform and its Consequences*, London: Rivers Oram Press.

Barnum, D.G. (1993) *The Supreme Court and American Democracy*, New York: St Martin's Press.

Bauman, Z. (1989) *Modernity and the Holocaust*, England: Polity Press.

Benn, C. and Chitty, C. (1996) *Thirty Years On: is comprehensive education alive and well or struggling to survive?* London: David Fulton.

Berube, M.R. (1994) *American School Reform: progressive, equity and excellence movements, 1883–1993*, Westport: Praeger.

Bettelheim, B. and Janowitz, M. (1950) *Dynamics of Prejudice*, New York: Harper.

Bhachu, P. (1984/6) 'Multicultural education: parental views', *New Community*, London: Commission for Racial Equality, 12, pp. 9–21.

Billig, M. (1976) *Social Psychology and Intergroup Relations*, London: Academic Press.

Billig, M. (1978) *Fascists: a social psychological view of the National Front*, London: Harcourt Brace Jovanich.

Billig, M. (1985) 'Prejudice, categorisation and particularisation: from a perceptual to a rhetorical approach', *European Journal of Social Psychology*, USA: Wiley, 15, pp. 79–103.

Billig, M. (1987) *Arguing and Thinking: a rhetorical approach to social psychology*, Cambridge: Cambridge University Press.

Bloom, H. (1994) *The Western canon: the books and school of the ages*, London: Harcourt.

Bowen, J. (1981) *A history of western education, Volume 3: the modern west*, London: Methuen.

Boyd-Barrett, O. (1995) 'Education and the languages of Spain', in Boyd-Barrett, O. and O'Malley, P. (eds) *Education reform in democratic Spain*, London: Routledge.

Boyd-Barrett, O. and O'Malley, P. (eds) (1995) *Education reform in democratic Spain*, London: Routledge.

Bracewell, W. (ed) (1991) 'National Identity in Eastern Europe and the Soviet Union: Special Issue', *Ethnic and Racial Studies*, London: Routledge, 14(1).

Brighouse, H. (2000) *Education equality and the new selective schooling*, Impact No. 3, England: Philosophy of Education Society of Great Britain.

Brogan, P. (1989) *World Conflicts: why and where they happen*, London: Bloomsbury.

Browning, G.R. (1992) *The Path to Genocide: essays on launching the final solution*, Cambridge: Cambridge University Press.

Bryk, A.S., Lee, V.E. and Holland, P.B. (1993) *Catholic schools and the common good*, Harvard: Harvard University Press.

Buckland, P. (1979) *The Factory of Grievances: devolved government in Northern Ireland 1921–1939*, Dublin: Gill and Macmillan.

Bullivant, B.M. (1992) 'The social realist case against affirmative action', in Lynch, J., Modgil, C. and Modgil, S. (eds) *Cultural Diversity and the Schools Volume One: education for cultural diversity: convergence and divergence*, England: Falmer Press.

Burbules, N.C. (1990) 'Equal opportunity or equal education?' *Educational Theory*, USA: University of Illinois at Urbana-Champaign, 40(2), pp. 221–226.

Burleigh, N. and Wippermann, W. (1991) *The Racial State: Germany 1933–1945*, Cambridge: Cambridge University Press.

Burns (2001) *Education for the 21st Century: report of the post primary review group*, Northern Ireland: Department of Education.

Cantle, T. (2001) *Community Cohesion: a report of the Independent Review Team*, London: Home Office.

Caplan, R. and Feffer, J. (1996) *Europe's New Nationalism: states and minorities in conflict*, Oxford: Oxford University Press.

Caportorti, F. (1991) *Study on the rights of persons belonging to ethnic, religious and linguistic minorities*, New York: United Nations.

CCEA (1997) *Mutual understanding and cultural understanding: cross-curricular guidance material*, Belfast: Council for the Curriculum, Examinations and Assessment.

Chalk, F. and Jonassohn, K. (1990) *The History and Sociology of Genocide: Analyses and Case Studies*, USA: Yale University Press.

Chirot, D. and Seligman, M.E.P. (eds) (2001) *Ethnopolitical Warfare: causes, consequences and possible solutions*, Washington DC: American Psychological Association.

Christie, P. (1991) *The Right to Learn: the struggle for education in South Africa*, South Africa: SACHED/Raven Press.

Christie, P. (1995) 'Transition tricks? policy models for school desegregation in South Africa, 1990–94', *Journal of Education Policy*, London: Taylor and Francis, 10(1), pp. 45–55.

Churchill, S. (1996) 'The decline of the nation state and the education of national minorities', *International Review of Education*, Netherlands: Kluwer, 42(4), pp. 265–290.

Churchill, W. (1929) *The World Crisis: the aftermath*, London: Odhams Press.

Clarke, T. (2001) *Report of the Burnley Task Force*, England: Burnley Task Force.

Clinton, B. (1995) *Remarks by the President on affirmative action, The Rotunda, National Archives, July 19, 1995*, Washington DC: Office of the Press Secretary, The White House.

Coard, B. (1971) 'How the West Indian Child is made ESN in the British School System', *New Teacher*, London: New Beacon Books, 8(4).

Cohn, E. (1997) *Market approaches to education: vouchers and school choice*, Oxford: Pergamon.

Connor, W. (1972) 'Nation-building or nation-destroying?' *World Politics*, 1972, USA: John Hopkins University Press, 24, pp. 319–355.

Cormack, R.J. and Osborne, R.D. (eds) (1983) *Religion, Education and Employment*, Belfast: Appletree Press.

Cormack, R.J. and Osborne, R.D. (eds) (1991) *Discrimination and Public Policy in Northern Ireland*, Oxford: Clarendon.

Coulby, D. (1997) 'Educational responses to diversity within the state', in Coulby, D. et al. (eds) *Intercultural Education: World Yearbook of Education 1997*, London: Kogan Page.

Coulby, D., Gundara, J. and Jones, C. (eds) (1997) *Intercultural Education: World Yearbook of Education 1997*, London: Kogan Page.

Craft, M. (ed) (1996) *Teacher Education in Plural Societies: an international review*, London: Falmer.

Cronin, A. (1983/4) 'Supplementary schools: their role in culture maintenance identity and underachievement', *New Community*, London: Commission for Racial Equality, 11, pp. 256–267.

Cumper, P. (1990) 'Muslim Schools: the implications of the Education Reform Act 1988', *New Community*, London: Commission for Racial Equality, 16(3), pp. 379–389.

Darby, J. (1991) *What's Wrong With Conflict?* Centre for the Study of Conflict Occasional Paper 3, Northern Ireland: University of Ulster.

Darby, J. (ed) (1983) *Northern Ireland: The Background to the Conflict*, Belfast: Appletree Press.

Darby, J. (1997) *Scorpions in a bottle: conflicting cultures in Northern Ireland*, London: Minority Rights Group.

Darby, J. and Dunn, S. (1987) 'Segregated Schools: The Research Evidence', in Osborne, R.D., Cormack, R.J. and Miller, R.L. (eds) *Education and Policy in Northern Ireland*, Belfast: Policy Research Institute.

Darby, J., Murray, D., Batts, D., Dunn, S., Farren, S. and Harris, J. (1977) *Education and Community in Northern Ireland: Schools Apart?* Coleraine: The New University of Ulster.

Davenport, T.R.H. (1998) *The birth of a new South Africa*, Canada: University of Toronto Press.

Davenport, R. and Saunders, C. (2000) *South Africa: a modern history*, London: Macmillan.

Davidson, B. (1985) *Africa in History: themes and outlines*, London: Paladin.

Davies, P. (ed) (1988) *Human Rights*, England: Routledge.

Day, A.J. (ed) (1986) *Peace Movements of the World: An International Directory: a Kessing's Reference Publication*, London: Longman.

Day, A.J. (ed) (1987) *Border and Territorial Disputes (2nd edition): a Kessing's Reference Publication*, London: Longman.

De Guchtenere, P., Le Duc, L. and Niemi, R.G. (1991) 'A Compendium of Academic Survey Studies of Elections Around the World, Update 1', *Electoral Studies*, Netherlands: Elsevier, 10(3), pp. 231–243.

Degenhardt, H.W. (ed) (1988) *Revolutionary and Dissident Movements: an International Guide, A Kessing's Reference Publication*, London: Longman.

DFES (2003) *Statistics of education: schools in England, 2003 edition*, London: National Statistics.

Dolan, J. (1982/3) 'Multicultural education for whom?' *New Community*, London: Commission for Racial Equality, Vol. 10, pp. 432–434.

Donald, J. (1985) 'Beacons of the future: schooling, subjection and subject-ification', in Beechey, V. and Donald, J. (eds) *Subjectivity and Social Relations*, Milton Keynes: Open University Press.

Davenport, T.R.H. (1998) *The birth of a new South Africa*, Canada: University of Toronto Press.

Dougherty, K.J. and Sostre, L. (1992) 'Minerva and the Market: the sources of the movement for school choice', in Cookson, P.W. (ed) *The Choice Controversy*, California: Corwin Press.

Dunant, S. (1994) *The war of the words: the political correctness debate*, London: Virago.

Dunn, S. (1990) 'A short history of education in Northern Ireland, 1920–1990, Annex B', *Fifteenth Report of the Standing Advisory Commission on Human Rights*, HC 459, London: HMSO.

Dunn, S. and Fraser, T. (eds) (1996) *Europe and ethnicity: World War I and contemporary ethnic conflict*, London: Routledge.

Dunn, S. and Smith, A. (1989) *Inter School Links*, Coleraine: University of Ulster.

Dunn, S., Darby, J. and Mullan, K. (1984) *Schools Together?* Coleraine: University of Ulster.

Edwards, J. (1995) *Affirmative action in a sectarian society: fair employment policy in Northern Ireland*, Aldershot: Avebury.

Esman, M.J. (1990) 'Political and Psychological Factors in Ethnic Conflict', in Montville, J. (ed) *Conflict and Peacemaking in Multiethnic Societies*, USA: Lexington Books.

Esteve, J.M. (1992) 'Multicultural education in Spain: the Autonomous Communities face the challenge of European unity', *Educational Review*, England: Carfax, 44(3), pp. 255–272.

Feinberg, W. (1998) *Common schools/Uncommon identities: national unity and cultural difference*, Yale: Yale University Press.

Fenton, S. (1982/3) 'Multi-something education', *New Community*, London: Commission for Racial Equality, Vol. 10, pp. 57–63.

Ferrer, F. (2000) 'Languages, minorities and education in Spain: the case of Catalonia', *Comparative Education*, England: Carfax, 36(2), pp. 187–197.

Fife, B. (1992) *Desegregation in American schools: comparative intervention strategies*, New York: Praeger.

Fitzgerald, R., Finch, S. and Nove, A. (2000) *Black Caribbean young men's experiences of education and employment, Research Report 186*, London: Department for Education and Employment.

Fitzmaurice, J. (1996) *The politics of Belgium: a unique federalism*, London: Hurst & Co.

Flecha, R. (1999) 'Modern and postmodern racism in Europe: dialogic approach and anti-racist pedagogies', *Harvard Educational Review*, Harvard: Harvard University Press, 69(2), pp. 150–171.

Fleming, G. (1985) *Hitler and the final solution*, London: Hamish Hamilton.

Focus (1997) *Who's Who in EMU?* Belfast: Forum for Community Understanding in Schools.

Forgey, H., Jeffery, A., Sidiropoulos, E., Smith, C., Corrigan, T., Mophuthing, T., Helman, A., Redpath, J. and Dimant, T. (1999) *South Africa Survey 1999/2000 Millennium Edition*, Johannesburg: South African Institute of Race Relations.

Foster, R.F. (1988) *Modern Ireland, 1600–1972*, London: Allen Lane.

Franklin, J.H. (1994) *Reconstruction after the Civil War*, Chicago: University of Chicago Press.

Fraser, R.M. (1973) *Children in Conflict*, London: Secker and Wartburg.

Gallagher, A.M. (1994) 'Political Discourse in a Divided Society', in Guelke, A. (ed) *New Perspectives on the Northern Ireland Conflict*, Aldershot: Avebury.

Gallagher, A.M. (1995a) 'The approach of government: community relations and equity', in Dunn, S. (ed) *Facets of the Conflict in Northern Ireland*, London/New York: Macmillan/St Martin's Press.

Gallagher, A.M. (1995b) 'Equity, contact and pluralism: attitudes to community relations', in Breen, R., Devine, P. and Robinson, G. (eds) *Social Attitudes in Northern Ireland*, Belfast: Appletree Press.

Gallagher, A.M. (1996) 'The Enduring Legacy: Reflections on Versailles', in Dunn, S. and Fraser, T. (eds) *Europe and Ethnicity*, London: Routledge.

Gallagher, A.M., Cormack, R.J. and Osborne, R.D. (1994) 'Religion, equity and education in Northern Ireland', *British Educational Research Journal*, England: Carfax, 20(5), pp. 507–518.

Gallagher, A.M., Osborne, R.D., Cormack, R.J., McKay, I. and Peover, S. (1995) 'Hazelwood Integrated College', in National Commission for Education (ed) *Success Against the Odds: effective schools in disadvantaged areas*, London: Routledge.

Gallagher, T. (2003) 'Education and equality in Northern Ireland', in Hargie, O. and Dickson, D. (eds) *Researching the Troubles: social science perspectives on the Northern Ireland conflict*, Edinburgh: Mainstream Publishing.

Gallagher, T. and Smith, A. (2001) 'The effects of selective education in Northern Ireland', *Education Review*, England: National Union of Teachers, 15(1), pp. 74–81

Gallagher, T., Smith, A. and Montgomery, A. (2003) *Integrated education in Northern Ireland: participation, profile and performance*, Coleraine: UU UNESCO Centre.

Garcia, A. (1991) 'Dispute Resolution Without Disputing', *American Sociological Review*, USA: American Sociological Society, 56(6), pp. 818–835.

Garrow, D.J. (1993) *Bearing the Cross: Martin Luther King Jr, and the Southern Christian Leadership Conference*, London: Vintage.

Giddens, A. (1989) *Sociology*, London: Polity Press.

Gilborn, D. (1997) 'Natural selection: New Labour, race and education policy', *Multicultural Teaching*, England: Trentham Books, 15(3), pp. 5–7.

Gilborn, D. and Gipps, C. (1996) *Recent research on the achievements of ethnic minority pupils*, OFSTED Reviews of Research, London: OFSTED.

Gilborn, D. and Mirza, H.S. (2000) *Educational inequality: mapping race, class and gender: a synthesis of research*, London: OFSTED.

Gilmour, J.D. (2001) 'Intention or in tension? Recent education reforms in South Africa', *International Journal of Educational Development*, Netherlands: Elsevier, 21, pp. 5–19.

Gilroy, P. (1992) 'The end of antiracism', in Donald, J. and Rattansi, A. (eds), *Race, Culture and Difference*, London: Sage.

Glazar, N. (1975) *Affirmative discrimination: ethnic inequality and public policy*, New York: Basic Books.

Glazar, N. and Moynihan, D.P. (1975) *Ethnicity: Theory and Experience*, England: Harvard University Press.

Glazar, N. and Young, K. (eds) (1983) *Ethnic Pluralism and Public Policy*, London: Heinemann.

Glazar, N. (1997) *We are all multiculturalists now*, Harvard: Harvard University Press.

Glenny, M. (1992) *The Fall of Yugoslavia: the third Balkan War*, Harmondsworth: Penguin.

Goble, P. (1989) 'Ethnic Politics in the USSR', *Problems of Communism*, Washington DC: US Information Agency, 38(4), pp. 1–14.

Gordon, L., Blignaut, S., Moroney, M. and Cooper, C. (1978) *A survey of race relations in South Africa*, Johannesburg: South African Institute of Race Relations.

Grant, N. (ed) (1988) 'Education and Minority Groups: Special Issue', *Comparative Education*, England: Carfax, 24(2).

Gretler, A. (1995) 'Switzerland', in Postlethwaite, T.N. (ed) *International Encyclopedia of National Systems of Education*, Oxford: Elsevier.

Groom, A.J.R. (1991) 'A Dip Into the Conflict Researcher's Toolbag', in Darby, J. and Gallagher, A.M. (eds) *Comparative Approaches to Community Conflict*,

Centre for the Study of Conflict Occasional Paper 4, Northern Ireland: University of Ulster.

Gutman, A. (1987) *Democratic Education*, Princeton: Princeton University Press.

Hanson, E.M. (2000) *Democratization and Educational Decentralization in Spain: A Twenty Year Struggle for Reform*, Country Studies: Education Reform and Management Publication Series, Washington DC: World Bank, Vol. 1, No. 3.

Harding, J. (1993) *Small Wars, Small Mercies: journeys in Africa's disputed nations*, London: Viking.

Hardy, J. and Vieler-Porter, C. (1992) 'Race, schooling and the 1988 Education Reform Act', in Gill, D., Mayor, B. and Blair, M. (eds) *Racism and Education: structures and strategies*, London: Sage.

Harvard Educational Review (1988) 'Race, Racism and American Education: Perspectives of Asian Americans, Blacks, Latinos and Native Americans: Special Issue', *Harvard Educational Review*, Harvard: Harvard University Press, 58(3).

Hatcher, R. (1997) 'New Labour, school improvement and racial equality', *Multicultural Teaching*, England: Trentham Books, 15(3), pp. 8–13.

Hatschikjan, M. (1991) 'Eastern Europe – Nationalist Pandemonium', Germany: Deutsche Verlags-Austalt, *Aussenpolitik*, 42(3), pp. 211–220.

Hawley, W.D. and Jackson, A.W. (eds) (1995) *Toward a Common Destiny: improving race and ethnic relations in America*, San Francisco: Josey-Bass.

Hega, G.M. (2001) 'Regional identity, language and education policy in Switzerland', *Compare*, England: Carfax, 31(2), pp. 205–227.

Herrez, J.C.G. (1995) 'Education in the state of Autonomous Communities', in Boyd-Barrett, O. and O'Malley, P. (eds) *Education reform in democratic Spain*, London: Routledge.

Heskin, K. (1980) *Northern Ireland: a psychological analysis*, Dublin: Gill and Macmillan.

Hilberg, R. (1985) *The Destruction of the European Jews*, New York: Holmes and Meier.

Hiro, D. (1992) *Black British White British: a history of race relations in Britain*, London: Paladin.

Hoare, Q. and Smith, G.H. (1971) *Antonio Gramsci: selections from prison notebooks*, London: Lawrence and Wishart.

Hobsbawm, E.J. (1994) *Age of Extremes: the short twentieth century 1914–1991*, London: Michael Joseph.

Hobsbawm, E.J. (1990) *Nations and Nationalism Since 1780*, England: Cambridge University Press.

Honig, J.W. and Both, N. (1996) *Srebrenica: record of a war crime*, Harmondsworth: Penguin.

Horowitz, D.L. (1990) 'Ethnic Conflict Management for Policymakers', in Montville, J. (ed) *Conflict and Peacemaking in Multiethnic Societies*, USA: Lexington Books.

Howe, K.R. (1989) 'In defense of outcomes-based conceptions of equal educational opportunity', *Educational Theory*, USA: University of Illinois at Urbana-Champaign, 39(4), pp. 317–336.

Howe, K.R. (1990) 'Equal opportunity is equal education (within limits)', *Educational Theory*, USA: University of Illinois at Urbana-Champaign, 40(2), pp. 227–230.

Howe, K.R. (1997) *Understanding equal educational opportunity: social justice, democracy and schooling*, New York: Teachers College Press.

Hughes, R. (1993) *Culture of Complaint: the fraying of America*, Oxford: Oxford University Press.

Ignatieff, M. (1994) *Blood and Belonging: journeys into the new nationalism*, London: Vintage.

Irwin, C. (1993) 'Making integrated education work for pupils', in Moffatt, C. (ed) *Education together for a change*, Belfast: Fortnight Educational Trust.

Jacobs, G.S. (1998) *Getting Round Brown: desegregation, development and the Columbus Public Schools*, USA: Ohio State University Press.

Jacoby, T. (1998) *Someone Else's House: America's unfinished struggle for integration*, New York: The Free Press.

James, A. (1982/3) 'What's wrong with multicultural education?', *New Community*, London: Commission for Racial Equality, 10, pp. 225–232.

Jansen, J.D. (1995) 'Understanding social transition through the lens of curriculum policy: Namibia/South Africa', *Journal of Curriculum Studies*, London: Taylor and Francis, 27(3), pp. 245–261.

Jencks, C. (1972) *Inequality: a reassessment of family and schooling in America*, New York: Basic Books.

Johnston, L. (2001) *The practice of integrated education in Northern Ireland: the teachers' perspective*, Research Report, Hofstra University, NY/Queen's University Belfast.

Kallen, D.B.P. and Sauthier, R. (1995) *Guide to secondary education in Europe*, Strasbourg: Council of Europe.

Karn, V. (ed) (1997) *Ethnicity in the 1991 Census, Volume 4: Employment, education and housing among the ethnic minority populations of Britain*, London: Office for National Statistics.

Karsten, S. (1994) 'Policy on ethnic segregation in a system of choice: the case of the Netherlands', *Journal of Education Policy*, London: Taylor and Francis, 9(3), pp. 211–225.

Keane, F. (1996) *Season of Blood: a Rwandan journey*, Harmondsworth: Penguin.

Kemerer, F.R. (2002) 'The US Supreme Court's decision in the Cleveland voucher case: here to from here?' *Occasional Paper No. 51, National Center for the Study of Privatization in Education*, Teachers College, Columbia University.

Kerner Commission (1968) *Report of the National Advisory Commission on Civil Disorders*, New York: Bantam Books.

Kershaw, I. (1984) *Popular Opinion and Political Dissent in the Third Reich: Bavaria 1933–1945*, Oxford: Oxford University Press.

Kidron, M. and Segal, R. (1984) *The New State of the World Atlas*, London: Pluto Press.

King, K. and McGrath, S. (2002) *Globalisation, enterprise and knowledge: education, training and development in Africa*, Oxford: Symposium Books.

Kliot, N. (1987) 'The Collapse of the Lebanese State', *Middle Eastern Studies*, London: Frank Cass, 23(1), pp. 54–74.

Kohn, M. (1995) *The Race Gallery*, London: Jonathon Cape.

Kolchin, P. (1993) *American Slavery*, Harmondsworth: Penguin.

Kozol, J. (1992) 'Inequality and the will to change', *Equity and Choice*, Boston: Institute for Responsive Education, 8(3), pp. 45–47.

Kuper, L. (1989) 'The prevention of genocide: cultural and structural indicators of genocidal threat', *Ethnic and Racial Studies*, London: Routledge, 12 (2), pp. 157–173.

Kymlicka, W. (1996) *The Rights of Minority Cultures*, Oxford: Oxford University Press.

Lane, J. and Ersson, S.O. (1994) *Politics and society in Western Europe*, London: Sage.

Lee, S. (1988) *Judging Judges*, London: Faber and Faber.

Leitch, R. and Kilpatrick, R. (1999) *Beyond the school gates: Strategies for supporting children's learning in primary and secondary schools: responding to cultures of political conflict*, Belfast: Save the Children Fund.

Lemann, N. (1991) *The Promised Land: the great Black migration and how it changed America*, London: Papermac.

Lendavi, P. (1991) 'Yugoslavia without Yugoslavs: the roots of the crisis', *International Affairs*, London: Royal Institute of International Affairs, 67(2), pp. 251–261.

Lifton, R.J. (1986) *The Nazi Doctors: a study in the psychology of evil*, Macmillan: London (page references are to the 1987 Papermac edition).

Little, A. and Robbins, D. (1982) *Loading the Law: A Study of Transmitted Deprivation, Ethnic Minorities and affirmative Action*, London: Commission for Racial Equality.

Little, A. (1984/6) 'Education for whom?', *New Community*, London: Commission for Racial Equality, 12, pp. 228–231.

Litvinoff, B. (1989) *The Burning Bush: antisemitism and world history*, London: Fontana.

Lomotey, K. and Teddlie, C. (eds) (1996) *Forty years after the Brown decision: implications of school desegregation for US education, Readings on Equal Education, Vol. 13*, New York: AMS Press.

MacKinnon, D., and Stratham, J. with Hales, M. (1995) *Education in the UK: facts and figures*, England: Open University Press.

MacPherson, W. (1999) *The Stephen Lawrence Inquiry*, Cm 4262–I, London: The Stationery Office.

Magee, J. (1970) 'The Teaching of Irish History in Irish Schools', *The Northern Teacher*, Belfast: Irish National Teachers' Organisation, 1970, 10(1), pp. 15–21.

Malone, J. (1973) 'Schools and Community Relations', *The Northern Teacher*, Belfast: Irish National Teachers' Organisation, 11(1), pp. 19–30,

Marrus, M.R. (1988) *The Holocaust in History*, London: Weidenfeld and Nicolson.

McCarthy, C. (1991) 'Multicultural Approaches to Racial Inequality in the United States', *Oxford Review of Education*, London: Carfax, 17(3), pp. 301–316.

McCrudden, C. (1986) 'Rethinking positive action', *Industrial Law Journal*, Oxford: Oxford University Press, 15, pp. 219–243.

McCrudden, C. (1992) 'Affirmative action and fair participation: interpreting the Fair Employment Act 1989', *Industrial Law Journal*, Oxford: Oxford University Press, 21 (3), p. 184.

McCrudden, C. (1996) 'The merit principle and fair employment in Northern Ireland', in Magill, D. and Rose, S. (eds) *Fair Employment in Northern Ireland: debates and issues*, Belfast: Standing Advisory Commission on Human Rights.

McDowell, D. (1992) *The Kurds: a Nation Denied*, London: Minority Rights Group.

McEwen, A. and Salters, J. (1993) Integrated Education: The Views of Parents in R. Osborne, R. Cormack and A. Gallagher (eds) *After the Reforms: Education and Policy in Northern Ireland,* Aldershot: Avebury.

McGonigle, J., Smith, A. and Gallagher, T. (2003) *Integrated education in Northern Ireland: the challenge of transformation,* Coleraine: UU UNESCO Centre.

McKeever, R.J. (1997) *The United States Supreme Court: a political and legal analysis,* Manchester: Manchester University Press.

McKernan, J. (1982) 'Constraints on the handling of Controversial Issues in Northern Ireland Post-Primary Schools', *British Educational Research Journal,* London: Carfax, 8(1), pp. 57–71.

McMullan, C. (2003) *A bridge or an island? An ethnographic study of an integrated school in Northern Ireland,* Unpublished PhD thesis, Queen's University Belfast.

McQuillan, P.J. and Donato, R. (1999) *Learning from history or repeating history: a preliminary examination of the return to segregated schools,* Paper presented to the Annual conference of the American Educational Research Association (AERA), Montreal.

Metz, M.H. (1986) *Different by design: the content and character of three magnet schools,* New York: Routledge, Keegan and Paul.

Miles, R. and Singer-Kerel, J. (eds) (1991) 'Migration and Migrants in France: Special Issue', *Ethnic and Racial Studies,* London: Carfax, 14(3).

Milliken, J. and Gallagher, T. (1998) 'Three Rs – religion, ritual and rivalry: strategic planning for integrated education in Northern Ireland', *Educational Management and Administration,* London: Sage, 26(4), pp. 443–456.

Milner, D. (1982/3) 'Multiculturalism: the "acceptable" face of multiracial education', *New Community,* London: Commission for Racial Equality, 10, pp. 72–75.

Minority Rights Group (1994) *Education rights and minorities,* London: Minority Rights Group.

Modgil, S., Verma, G.K., Mallick, K. and Modgil, C. (eds) (1986) *Multicultural Education: The Interminable Debate,* England: The Falmer Press.

Moffat, C. (ed) (1993) *Education Together for a Change,* Belfast: Fortnight Educational Trust.

Mommsen, H. (1986) 'The Realization of the Unthinkable: the "Final Solution of the Jewish Question" in the Third Reich', in Hirchfeld, G. (ed) *The Politics of Genocide: Jews and Soviet Prisoners of War in Nazi Germany,* London: Allan and Unwin.

Montville, J. (ed) (1990) *Conflict and Peacemaking in Multiethnic Societies,* USA: Lexington Books.

Morgan, V., Fraser, G., Dunn, S. and Cairns, E. (1992a) Parental Involvement in Education: How do parents want to become involved? *Educational Studies,* 18(1), London: Carfax, pp. 11–20.

Morgan, V., Dunn, S., Cairns, E. and Fraser, G. (1992b) *Breaking the Mould: The Roles of Parents and Teachers in the Integrated Schools in Northern Ireland,* Centre for the Study of Conflict, Coleraine: University of Ulster.

Motala, S. (2001) 'Quality and indicators of quality in South African education: a critical appraisal', *International Journal of Educational Development,* Netherlands: Kluwer, 21, pp. 61–78.

Mullard, C. (1985) 'Multicultural education in Britain: from assimilation to cultural pluralism', in Arnot, M. (ed) *Race and Gender: equal opportunities policies in education,* London: Pergamon Press.

Murray, D. (1983) 'Rituals and symbols as contributors to the culture of Northern Ireland primary schools', *Irish Educational Studies*, Dublin: Educational Studies Association of Ireland, 3(2), pp. 238–255.

Murray, D. (1985a) *Worlds Apart: segregated schools in Northern Ireland*, Belfast: Appletree Press.

Murray, D. (1985b) 'Identity: a covert pedagogy in Northern Irish schools', *Irish Educational Studies*, Dublin: Educational Studies Association of Ireland, 5(2), pp. 182–197,

Nakabugo, M.G. and Siebörger, R. (2001) 'Curriculum reform and teaching in South Africa: making a paradigm shift?' *International Journal of Educational Development*, Netherlands: Kluwer, 21, pp. 53–60.

Naimark, N.M. (2001) *Fires of Hatred: ethnic cleansing in twentieth-century Europe*, Harvard: Harvard University Press.

Nash, G.B., Crabtree, C. and Dunn, R.E. (2000) *History on trial: culture wars and the teaching of the past*, New York: Vintage.

Nicholson, H. (1933) *Peacemaking 1919*, London: Constable.

Nixon, J. (1984/6) 'Multicultural education as a curriculum category', *New Community*, London: Commission for Racial Equality, 12, pp. 22–30.

Noakes, J. and Pridham, G. (eds) (1983) *Nazism 1919–1945, Volume 1: The Rise to Power 1991–1934*, England: Exeter University Publications.

Noakes, J. and Pridham, G. (eds) (1984) *Nazism 1919–1945, Volume 2: State, Economy and Society 1933–1939*, England: Exeter University Publications.

Noakes, J. and Pridham, G. (eds) (1986) *Nazism 1919–1945, Volume 3: Foreign Policy, War and Racial Extermination*, England: Exeter University Publications.

Norkvelle, Y. (1995) 'Teachers, culture and politics: the struggle for a curriculum for the free Namibia, A case study of the Namibia secondary school', *Journal of Education Policy*, London: Taylor and Francis, 10(4), pp. 361–371.

O'Connor, S. (1980) Reports – 'Chocolate Cream Soldiers: Evaluating an Experiment in Non-Sectarian Education in Northern Ireland', *Journal of Curriculum Studies*, London: Taylor and Francis, 12(3), pp. 263–270.

O'Connor, U., Hartop, B. and McCully, A. (2002) *A review of the schools community relations programme*, Northern Ireland; Department of Education.

OECD (1990) *Reviews of national policies for education: the Netherlands*, Paris: OECD.

OECD (1991) *Reviews of national policies for education: Switzerland*, Paris: OECD.

OECD (1993) *Reviews of national policies for education: Belgium*, Paris: OECD.

OECD (1994) *School: a matter of choice*, Paris: OECD.

OFSTED (1999) *Raising the attainment of minority ethnic pupils*, London: OFSTED.

Orfield, G. and Eaton, S. (1996) *Dismantling desegregation: the quiet reversal of Brown versus Board of Education*, New York: New Press.

Orfield, G. and Miller, E. (1998) *Chilling admissions: the affirmative action crisis and the search for alternatives*, Harvard: Harvard Education Publishing Group.

Orfield, G. and Yun, J.T. (1999) *Resegregation in American Schools*, Harvard Civil Rights Project: Harvard.

Osborne, R.D. and Cormack, R.J. (1987) *Religion, Occupations and Employment, 1971–81*, Belfast: Fair Employment Agency.

Osborne, R.D., Gallagher, A.M. and Cormack, R.J. (1989) 'Review of Aspects of Education in Northern Ireland, Annex H', *Fourteenth Annual Report of the Standing Advisory Commission on Human Rights*, London: HMSO.

Ouseley, H. (2001) *Community pride not prejudice: making diversity work in Bradford*, England: Bradford Vision.

Owen, D., Green, A., Pitcher, J. and Maguire, M. (2000) *Minority ethnic participation and achievements in education, training and the labour market, Research Report 225*, London: Department for Education and Employment.

Pakenham, T. (1982) *The Boer War*, London: Futura.

Pallas, A. (2002) 'Don't Believe the Hype: A Commentary on Zelman', *Teachers College Record*, http://www,tcrecord,org ID Number: 10969, Date Accessed: 8/28/02.

Parekh, B. (1992) 'The hermeneutics of the Swann Report', in Gill, D., Mayor, B. and Blair, M. (eds) *Racism and Education*, London: Sage.

Parekh Report (2000) *The future of multi-ethnic Britain: the Parekh Report*, London: Profile Books.

Parkin, F. (1979) 'Social Stratification', in Bottomore, T. and Nisbet, R. (eds) *A History of Sociological Analysis*, London: Heinemann Educational Books.

Pathak, S. (2000) *Race research for the future: ethnicity in education, training and the labour market, Research Topic Paper 1*, London: Department for Education and Employment.

Peang-Meth, A. (1991) 'Understanding the Khmer: sociological-cultural observations', *Asian Survey*, California: University of California Press, 31(5), pp. 442–455

Phillips, D. (ed.) (1991) 'Equality and Education Revisited: Special Issue', *Oxford Review of Education*, England: Carfax, 17(2).

Pluralism in Education (1996) *Pluralism in Education Conference Report*, Dublin: Dublin City University.

Polenberg, R. (1980) *One Nation Divisible: class, race and ethnicity in the United States since 1938*, Harmondsworth: Penguin.

Potter, J. and Wetherell, M. (1987) *Discourse and Social Psychology: beyond attitudes and behaviour*, London: Sage.

Poulton, H. (1991) *The Balkans: Minorities and States in Conflict*, London: Minority Rights Group.

Premdas, R.R. (1991) 'Fiji under a new political order: ethnicity and indigenous rights', *Asian Survey*, California: University of California Press, 31(6), pp. 540–558

Ra'anan, U. (1990) 'The Nation-State Fallacy', in Montville, J. (ed) *Conflict and Peacemaking in Multiethnic Societies*, USA: Lexington Books.

Raffel, J.A. (1998) *Historical Dictionary of school segregation and desegregation: the American experience*, Westport: Greenwood Press.

Ram, M. (1989) *Sri Lanka: the Fractured Island*, England: Penguin Books.

Rattansi, A. (1992) 'Changing the subject? Racism, culture and education', in Donald, J. and Rattansi, A. (eds) *'Race', Culture and Difference*, London: Sage.

Reardon, S.F., Yun, J.T. and Eitle, T.McN. (1999) 'The changing context of school segregation: measurement and evidence of multi-racial metropolitan area school segregation, 1989–1995', *Paper presented at the Annual Conference of the American Educational Research Association (AERA)*, Montreal.

Reich, R.B. (1991) 'What is a Nation?', *Political Science Quarterly*, USA: Academy of Political Science, 106(2), pp. 193–209.

Remarque, E.M. (1929) *All Quiet on the Western Front*, (1980 edition, London: Guild Publishing).

Rex, J. (1986) *Race and Ethnicity*, England: Open University Press.

Rex, J. and Mason, D. (eds) (1986) *Theories of Race and Ethnic Relations*, England: Cambridge University Press.

Richards, J.K. (1982/3) 'A contribution to the multicultural education debate', *New Community*, London: Commission for Racial Equality, 10, pp. 222–224.

Richmond, A.H. (1984/6) 'Before and after the Swann Report', *New Community*, London: Commission for Racial Equality, 12, pp. 225–227.

Richmond, A.H. (1987) 'Ethnic nationalism: social science paradigms', *International Social Science Journal*, Paris: UNESCO, 111, pp. 3–18.

Ritchie, D. (2001) *Panel Report: Oldham Independent Review*, England: Oldham Independent Review.

Rupesinghe, K. and Tishkov, V.A. (1996) *Ethnicity and power in the contemporary world*, Tokyo: United Nations University Press.

SACHR (1985) *Religious and Political Discrimination and Equality of Opportunity in Northern Ireland: Report on Fair Employment*, London: HMSO.

SACHR (1989) *Fourteenth Report of the Standing Advisory Commission on Human Rights*, London: HMSO.

SACHR (1990) *Fifteenth Report of the Standing Advisory Commission on Human Rights*, London: HMSO.

SACHR (1991) *Sixteenth Report of the Standing Advisory Commission on Human Rights*, London: HMSO.

SACHR (1992) *Seventeenth Report of the Standing Advisory Commission on Human Rights*, London: HMSO.

Said, E.W. (1978) *Orientalism: Western concepts of the Orient*, Harmondsworth: Penguin.

Saroyan, M. (1990) 'The Karabakh Syndrome and Azerbaijani Politics', *Problems of Communism*, Washington DC: US Information Agency, 39(5), pp. 14–29

Saunders, M. (1982/3) 'Education for a new community', *New Community*, London: Commission for Racial Equality, Vol. 10, pp. 64–71.

Schlesinger, A.M. (1978) *Robert Kennedy and His Times*, New York: Ballantine Books.

Schlesinger, A.M. (1991) *The disuniting of America: reflections on a multicultural society*, New York: Whittle Books.

Seybolt, T.B. (2000) 'Major Armed Conflicts', in SIPRI, *Yearbook 2000: Armaments, Disarmament and International Security*, Oxford: Oxford University Press.

Seybolt, T.B. (2002) 'Major Armed Conflicts', in SIPRI *Yearbook 2002: Armaments, Disarmament and International Security*, Oxford: Oxford University Press.

Sherif, M. (1966) *Group conflict and cooperation: their social psychology*, London: Routledge and Kegan Paul.

Sherif, M., Harvey, O.J., White, J., Hood, W.R. and Sherif, C.W. (1961) *Intergroup Conflict and Cooperation: The Robbers Cave Experiment*, Norman, OK: Book Exchange

Shirer, W. (1959) *The Rise and Fall of the Third Reich*, London: Secker and Warburg.

Silber, L. and Little, A. (1996) *The Death of Yugoslavia*, revised edition, Harmondsworth: Penguin.

SIPRI (2002) *SIPRI Yearbook 2002: Armaments, Disarmament and International Security*, Oxford: Oxford University Press.

Skilbeck, M. (1973) 'The School and Cultural Development', *The Northern Teacher*, Belfast: Irish National Teachers' Organisation, 11(1), pp. 13–18,

Smith, A. and Dunn, S. (1990) *Extending Inter-School Links*, Coleraine: University of Ulster.

Smith, A. and Robinson, A. (1992) *Education for Mutual Understanding: Perceptions and Policy*, Coleraine: University of Ulster.

Smith, A. and Robinson, A. (1996) *EMU: the initial statutory years*, Coleraine: University of Ulster.

Smith, A.D. (1991) *National Identity*, Harmondsworth: Penguin Books.

Social Exclusion Unit (1998) *Truancy and school exclusion: report by the Social Exclusion Unit, Cm 3957*, London: The Stationery Office.

Sollenberg, M. and Wallensteen, P. (1995) 'Major Armed Conflicts', in *SIPRI Yearbook 1995: Armaments, Disarmament and International Security*, Oxford: Oxford University Press.

Sollenberg, M. and Wallensteen, P. (1998) 'Major Armed Conflicts', in *SIPRI Yearbook 1998: Armaments, Disarmament and International Security*, Oxford: Oxford University Press.

Sollenberg, M., Wallensteen, P. and Jato, A. (1999) 'Major Armed Conflicts', in *SIPRI Yearbook 1999: Armaments, Disarmament and International Security*, Oxford: Oxford University Press.

Sollenberg, M. and Wallensteen, P. (2001) 'Appendix 1A: Major Armed Conflicts', in *SIPRI Yearbook 2001: armaments, disarmament and international security*, Oxford: Oxford University Press.

Solomos, J. (1992) 'The politics of immigration since 1945', in Braham, P., Rattansi, A. and Skellington, R. (eds) *Racism and Antiracism: inequalities, opportunities and policies*, London: Sage.

Soudien, C. (2001) 'Teachers' responses to rationalisation: transformation and adaptation in the Western Cape, South Africa', *International Journal of Educational Development*, Netherlands: Kluwer, 21, pp. 33–43.

Spear, A.H. (1967) *Black Chicago: the making of a negro ghetto*, Chicago: Chicago University Press.

Spencer, A.E.C.W. (1987) 'Arguments for an Integrated School System', in Osborne, R.D., Cormack, R.J. and Miller, R.L. (eds), *Education and Policy in Northern Ireland*, Belfast: Policy Research Institute.

Spencer, J. (1990) 'Collective violence and everyday practice in Sri Lanka', *Modern Asian Studies*, Cambridge: Cambridge University Press, 24(3), pp. 603–623.

Staub, E. (1989) *The Roots of Evil: The Origins of Genocide and Other Group Violence*, England: Cambridge University Press.

Stavenhagen, R. (1991) *The Ethnic Question*, Japan: United Nations University.

Stent, M. (1994) 'The pillars of apartheid', in Harker, J. (ed) *The Legacy of Apartheid*, London: Guardian Newspapers.

Swann Report (1985) *Education For All*, London: HMSO.

Tajfel, H. (1970) 'Experiments in intergroup discrimination', *Scientific American*, USA: Verlagsgruppe Georg von Holtzbrink, 223, pp. 96–102.

Tajfel, H. (1972) 'Experiments in a vacuum', in Israel, J. and Tajfel, H. (eds) *The Context of Social Psychology*, London: Academic Press.

Tajfel, H. (1981) *Human groups and social categories: studies in social psychology*, Cambridge: Cambridge University Press.

Tajfel, H. (ed) (1984) *The Social Dimension: European Developments in Social Psychology Volume 2*, Cambridge: Cambridge University Press.

Tajfel, H. et al. (1971) 'Social categorisation and intergroup behaviour', *European Journal of Social Psychology*, USA: Wiley, 1, pp. 149–177.

Tarrow, N.B. (ed) (1987) *Human Rights and Education*, England: Pergamon Press.

Taylor, A. (1992) 'The Bond and Break Between Us', *English Education*, England: Conference on English Education, 26(3), pp. 24–30.

Taylor, W.T. (1990) 'Multi-cultural education in the white highlands after the 1988 Education Reform Act', *New Community*, London: Commission for Racial Equality, 16(3), pp. 369–378.

Thernstrom, S. and Thernstrom, A. (1997) *America in Black and White: One nation, indivisible*, New York: Simon and Schuster.

Thompson, M. (1992) *A Paper House: the ending of Yugoslavia*, London: Vintage.

Tikley, L. (1997) 'Changing South African schools? an analysis and critique of post-election government policy', *Journal of Education Policy*, London: Taylor and Francis, 12(3), pp. 177–188.

Timmins, N. (1996) *The Five Giants: a biography of the welfare state*, England: Fontana Press.

Tindall, G.B. and Shi, D.E. (1999) *America: a narrative history*, USA: Norton.

Tollet, K.S. (1982) 'The propriety of the federal role in expanding equal educational opportunity', *Harvard Educational Review*, Harvard: Harvard University Press, 52(4), pp. 431–443.

Tomlinson, S. (1982/3) 'The educational performance of children of Asian origin', *New Community*, London: Commission for Racial Equality, 10, pp. 381–392.

Tomlinson, S. (1985) 'The Black Education movement', in Arnot, M. (ed) *Race and Gender: equal opportunities policies in education*, London: Pergamon Press.

Tomlinson, S. (1996) 'Teacher education for a multicultural Britain', in Craft, M. (ed) *Teacher education in plural societies: an international review*, London: Falmer.

Tomlinson, S. (1997) 'Diversity, choice and ethnicity: the effects of educational markets on ethnic minorities', *Oxford Review of Education*, England: Carfax, 23(1), pp. 63–76.

Troyna, B. (1982/3) 'Multiracial education: just another brick in the wall?', *New Community*, London: Commission for Racial Equality, Vol. 10, pp. 424–428.

Troyna, B. (1990) 'Reform or deform? The 1988 Education Reform Act and racial equality in Britain', *New Community*, London: Commission for Racial Equality, 16(3), pp. 403–416.

Troyna, B. (1992) 'Can you see the join? A historical analysis of multicultural and antiracist education policies', in Gill, D., Mayor, B. and Blair, M. (eds) *Racism and Education: structures and strategies*, London: Sage.

Tusa, A. and Tusa, J. (1983) *The Nuremburg Trial*, London: Macmillan.

US State Department (1998) *Patterns of global terrorism: 1997, Department of State Publication 10535*, Washington: US State Department.

Vally, S. (1998) *Inequality in education? Revisiting the provisioning, funding and governance of schooling*, Quarterly Review, 5(4), University of Witswatersrand: Education Policy Unit.

Vanderstraeten, R. (2002) 'Cultural values and social differentiation: the Catholic pillar and its education system in Belgium and the Netherlands', *Compare*, England: Carfax, 32(2), pp. 133–148.

Varshney, A. (2002) *Ethnic conflict and civic life: Hindus and Muslims in India*, Yale: Yale University Press.

Verhoeven, J. (1992) 'Key issues in educational policy for secondary schools in federated Belgium', *Journal of Education Policy*, London: Taylor and Francis, 7(1), pp. 99–107.

Walker, C.J. (1991) *Armenia and Karabagh: The Struggle for Unity*, London: Minority Rights Group.

Weiss, A. (1988) (ed) *Yad Vashem Studies*, Jerusalem: Yad Vashem Holocaust Martyrs' and Heroes Remembrance Authority, 19, pp. 1–186.

Wells, A.S. (2002) 'Reactions to the Supreme Court Ruling on Vouchers: Introduction to an Online Special Issue', *Teachers College Record*, http://www.tcrecord.org ID Number: 10949, Date Accessed: 8/28/02.

Wright, F. (1987) *Northern Ireland: a comparative analysis*, Dublin: Gill and Macmillan.

X, M. with Haley, A. (1966) *The autobiography of Malcolm X, as told to Alex Haley*, London: Hutchinson.

Young, J.N. (1984/6) 'ILEA's anti-racist policy: a note', *New Community*, London: Commission for Racial Equality, 12, pp. 31–32.

Index